# Cottage Witchcraft

## Jan McDonald

# www.capallbann.co.uk

# Cottage Witchcraft

Cover design by Paul Mason
Internal pictures by the author

Published by:

Capall Bann Publishing
Auton Farm
Milverton
Somerset
TA4 1NE

To Bill, husband, lover and best friend

# Contents

# Part One

# The Basics

## To the Cottage Witch Past and Present

*In days of superstition and dread, priestly fervour, now happily dead*

*The Witch's Craft both loved and feared, outlawed by man and not revered*

*Lived in secret in the gentle heart, and lives on still in the Witch's art.*

*Yet in those days of terror dark, her truth would bring a future stark.*


*The angry crowd took up the cry, 'Burn the witch! Let's watch her die!'*

*A mark from birth upon my side, convinced them all I'm the Devil's bride.*

*Yet I've cured them all of common ills, from fiery fevers to deathly chills,*

*I've helped in births and dressed their dead and now their terror and anger is fed*

*By a man who walks with head held high, who'll burn the witch and watch her die.*

*The pestilence was upon the child, her mind in fever and body defiled*

*'Help her now!' the mother's cry, 'Bring your herbs, don't let her die!'*

*No potion or brew would save or curb the plague within, but Willowherb*

*Would deaden the pain and give her ease but the Angel of Death would not appease.*

*And when she died they searched for blame, 'She's killed the child', the Man did claim.*

*'She's a Witch', he said, 'You all must learn, to torture the witches and watch them burn.*

*She suckles an imp! And I've seen her fly, so burn the witch and watch her die.'*


*Stabbed with blades and fiery brands, tortured and clawed with filthy hands*

*'Confess', they said, 'to being a witch, dancing with devils in hedge and ditch.*

*For listening to wind and talking to trees, a witch', they said, 'should hang in the breeze.'*

*They swam me deep in the village pond to see if my soul would travel beyond.*

*Drowned, my innocence would proclaim but living, surely would damn my name.*

*'We shall not suffer a witch to live, her sins and blasphemies not forgive.'*


*Amongst the crowd that screamed for death were faces of children I helped draw breath*

*Mothers whose labour I'd eased with care, others who'd come in pain and despair.*

*Features distorted with terror and hate, determined only to broker my fate.*

On a bonfire under the winter sky they'll burn the witch and watch her die.

A hand reached through the savage crowd, a hand of pity with love endowed
Secreted within, an herb of release to bring both swift and final peace.
Grateful to her for the blessed Dwale I passed through sleep to Death's own vale
And as the flames burned bright and high, they burned the witch and watched her die.
The Man moved on, his job well done, an evil quenched, a battle won.
Now he's gone and they're alone, no comfort now from the village crone.
And who will help their dying find peace? The children's pain and suffering release?
And who will break their fever's hold? Protect them all from winter's cold?
They're sorry now for that bonfire high, when they burned the witch and watched her die.

Now centuries past and the truth is known, no evil lives in the village crone
Just knowledge and love for her fellow man, though Governments foolish still would ban
The use of nature's bounty to heal, a broken heart, a festering wheal.
Though Science bold has shown them all that herbs have powers for us to call
But money rules the coldest heart, no profit found in the witch's art.
Power's loss is what fuels their fire, not mystery burned on the village pyre.

*When will they learn that the simple flower can show us all the meaning of power?*

*Laws will be passed to steal our art, and the witch again will hide her heart,*

*But the path to her door will always be trod, protected by both her Goddess and God.*

*Nature knows her gentle ways, and so she is blessed to the end of her days.*

# Foreword

This book is in direct response to many requests over the past few years for a book that cuts away all the excess fat from the bones of witchcraft. 'Give us something that is simple, something we can do even when we're tired, the kids are crying, the dog's muddy paw prints are all over the floor and the mother-in-law is coming round for tea. We want something that's meaningful and special without the added extras. We don't have the time or the energy for tramping around fields looking for special herbs or the money for great lists of equipment and rare herbs from occult suppliers.'

That is precisely what Cottage Witchcraft is all about. A simple approach to the Old Goddesses and Gods and making magic from everyday objects and what is available in everyday living without the need for ceremonial tools and equipment or robes. I realise that some witches will not agree, but hey, that's okay, it works for me and I'm sure it will work for you. So here it is.

Whilst many of today's witches opt to practice their craft amongst likeminded folk in a coven situation, a growing number prefer the way of the solitary witch. This book is intended purely as a signpost to those embarking on this path and will hopefully simplify the business of magic and show that when all is said and done, none of us is truly alone.

The great thing about signposts is that you can follow them directly to your destination or wander off the path and explore beautiful country along the way. The spontaneous meandering from the signed road can often lead to unexpected delights like a magical glade and crystal streams. Take a walk with me up the old pathway to the door of the cottage witch and enter her realm of natural magic and the Old Religion.

Let's stir the bubbling cauldron and set free the magic in you. It's easy, come with me.

# 1. Introduction to the Cottage Witch

*The door is always open to her kitchen warm and bright,*
*She'll listen to your troubles be it day, or be it night.*
*Her cat sleeps by her fireside, contented warm and fed*
*As she casts a spell of plenty while she bakes her daily bread.*
*Fairies dance around her while she weaves her magick cloak,*
*To sit around her shoulders as she gathers moss of oak.*
*Her cauldrons always bubbling on her hearth of rough hewn stone,*
*A witch in name and nature from childhood through to crone.*

## What is cottage witchcraft?

The way of the witch calls to the soul of so many of us, but the simple fact is that in today's hectic world, with careers, families and other responsibilities most don't have the time or at the end of a busy day are just too tired for elaborate rites and rituals or a journey to coven meetings yet there is a yearning to respond to this primal need. Others simply prefer to work alone. Sound familiar?

Cottage witchcraft goes back to the days when many witches lived alone in rural surroundings with little or no resources other than those that nature provided and in some ways this becomes witchcraft in one of its pure forms. During the times of persecution witches were afraid to broadcast their beliefs and practices and very often had no contact with others like them. The art of the solitary witch is simple and straightforward yet no less powerful coming as it does from the heart. It can be planned or spontaneous and it brings with it a sense of peace and meaning into today's whirlwind of living.

In days gone by the witch in her cottage at the edge of the village practiced her art at her hearthside. Her tools weren't purchased from expensive magical supply stores and her 'recipes' were passed down from generation to generation verbally, she had no access to books as we have today and if she could write she would keep a handwritten record to be passed on. She used what was to hand and was extremely practical, usually out of need. She was a nurse, a cook, a wise woman and healer. She made nourishing food from what she could obtain near her own front door, from what was seasonal and fresh or what she had been able to preserve and store throughout the winter months. She probably had a far healthier diet than many of us today and fed her family with the magic of her love and care. She knew nature, lived in tune with the changing seasons and used her own energies for her own brand of magic. A magic that worked and can do today.

It is so easy for us with the out of town superstores and high street supermarkets to eat strawberries in December and our centrally heated homes blend one season into another. Whilst this enables us to structure our busy lifestyle for today's demands, our psyches still respond to the changing seasons and the natural cycles of life. Cottage witchcraft brings them back into focus in a gentle and logical way.

I am not suggesting for one moment that we return to cold drafty houses and shun the modern developments that enable us to live safely and comfortably in today's world, but maybe, occasionally, we can find the time to visit local markets and buy food that is seasonal, to wrap up and take a walk in the cold frosty air instead of curling up in front of the TV, watch the cycles of the moon and be in touch once again with the natural forces that surround us.

Anyone can practice Cottage Witchcraft, you don't have to live in a chocolate box cottage at the edge of a wood, although some of us may be that lucky, it is the essence of the cottage witch that speaks to us all in our town houses, high rise apartments, housing estates, bungalows, caravans and boats. Our homes can once again come alive and vibrate with her magic and our lives be enchanted by her powers. They come from within and are echoed down the centuries to emerge as a valid and powerful energy. Casting a spell can be as uncomplicated as making a cup of tea.

Her essence is in simplicity as is her magic. Remember – Kiss ( **K**eep *I*t **S**imple **S**weetie)!

So if her spirit is calling to you, read on and enter the magical world of the cottage witch. May she be forever blessed.

# 2. The Goddess and the God

*She's the Maiden, the Mother, the Crone and the Shade*
*She's in tempest and meadow and cool forest glade.*
*He leads the Wild Hunt on the darkest of night*
*He's the stag in the forest, the Eagle in flight.*
*Together they reign in magick and love*
*Mystical union of hawk and the dove.*

Why a Goddess and God? Why not just magic?

Because the spiritual enhancement that they give us helps to attune us to the forces of nature that we are about to use in magic. Spellcasting is simply using the energies that are in and around us and directing those energies outward to bring about a desired change. It makes sense then to be aware of and respect those energies or forces that make this possible.

Throughout all creation there is a female and male principle, without one or the other there can be no new life. The Old Religion honour both in the forms of a Goddess and a God, female and male in balance, both equally important but bearing very different roles.

The Goddess has many faces and many names; all are relevant and speak to us at different times in our lives. As the principle of Cottage Witchcraft is simplicity I shall refer to her simply as The Lady. She may speak to you with the voice of any of the Goddesses and that will be between you and Her, you will know it when she shows her face to you. She speaks to me as Hecate, the Goddess of the Underworld, the crone, the Goddess of the crossroads, to you she may be Persephone, Diana or any of her other aspects. It is important to remember that all of the faces are just one manifestation of the same Goddess. She is Mother Earth, she reflects her phases in the Moon, she is the cool waters of the crystal rivers and streams, she nurtures and heals. She is ever present and ever changing.

The God of The Old Religion is seen as The Horned God, the rutting stag, the leader of the Wild Hunt, protector and bringer of change. He challenges us out of our comfortable lives to seek movement, change and innovation. He too has many names and faces though usually known in these isles as Herne the Hunter, the Lord of the Greenwood. He is the consort of the Goddess and may simply be known as The Lord. I have often addressed Him as Sir.

The Goddess and God together form the patterns of our lives and these are reflected in their story as the year unfolds, as can be seen in the chapter Seasons and Celebrations. One thing is certain; words cannot succeed in describing them fully. They cannot be rationalised, only experienced, they are part of the Mystery.

The Goddess has four phases as does the Moon. We can see Her in Her youth as the Maiden, in Middle Age as the Mother, in old age as the Crone and in death as the Dark Goddess, reflected as the New Moon, Full Moon, Waning Moon and the Dark of the Moon. Many witches prefer to think of Her as threefold, the Maid, Mother and Crone, but I can't help but feel that this misses the point of the circle of life when it is the Dark Goddess that leads us to the Otherworld for rest and renewal before rebirth. But the beauty of the Craft is that it is all things to all people, no one interpretation of it is more or less valid than the other. As I have already said, we all see The Goddess and God differently, perhaps this is one of the points at which you may wish to wander from the signed road and see for yourself what lies just off the path.

In looking at other interpretations of The Old Religion, Wicca, The Craft, (you see how many different names there are for this wonder?) we need to remember that some of these 'versions' are imported from Europe, Italy for instance, where the Tuscan witches revered Aradia as their Goddess. There is no written script, no Bible, nothing laid down in stone, all are simply one idea which has been perpetuated, as indeed is this book. I believe that as solitary witches we have the creativity and intelligence to see for ourselves, speak for ourselves and honour the Goddess and God in our own way, as indeed the Cottage Witch would have done. Believe me, the Lady listens when we speak to her, in whatever language we choose. She answers to whichever name we give Her.

One thing I have found over the years is that both The Goddess and God have a profound capacity for laughter, just as well I guess when dealing with us humans. Never worry if a simple ritual or spellcasting goes wrong or backfires, or you mix up your words, just start over and listen for the laughter. A witch that has never made a mistake isn't a witch at all but superhuman. I am reminded of the time that I set my altar on fire (I have problems around the fire element!) with nothing to put it out but the wine in the chalice! They had a good laugh at that one I can tell you.

On the subject of initiation, I'm sure you have read of powerful ceremonies where initiation into the Mysteries is conferred on a new witch by a High Priest or High Priestess on behalf of the Goddess. For the Cottage Witch this happens internally, there is a point when you just 'know' you belong, it feels like coming home. In the spirit of simplicity there need be no ceremony as such, just a simple acknowledgement, or you may wish to carry out some form of self-dedication, if that is the case the signposts are out again, and a simple ritual of dedication appears later on in the chapter Rites and Rituals.

Acknowledgement of the Goddess and God on a daily basis need not be time consuming or elaborate, but is I feel, necessary. It can be as simple as 'Good morning my Lady, and you too, Sir' when you rise, or as you wash the breakfast dishes look out of your kitchen window and see what Mother Earth has laid at your doorstep. Even from the window of a high rise apartment we can see window boxes or the occasional tree and what of the hustle and bustle of others going about their daily 'rituals'? A simple thought of 'Thank you' is a powerful message and lighting the candles of your household altar for just five minutes each day helps you touch base with them. I will talk more of altars and sacred space later, but for now it is enough to say that paying a visit for just a few moments can be really uplifting.

It is the Goddess in you that picks up your crying child and cuddles her; it is the nurturer, the creative force. It's her that stirs your cooking pots and your paint pots. It's the God in you that says, 'Hey, time you had a new job, time to look for promotion. Time to do something'. The feminine and masculine energies are present in us all, male and female, and both are valid and of equal value but very different from each other. It is a mistake to think that to allow the gentle, nurturing Goddess to have free rein means that we are weaker than our men, we're just different and we are meant to be that way. There is much criticism of stereotypes and sexism, but you know, women really are meant to be the gentler sex, the nurturers, the creative, caring. Viva la difference!

During the later chapters you will see those signposts again, as I give you some ideas for rituals to the Goddess and God, use them as they are for a while, until you devise your own way or go for it from the outset, it's entirely up to you.

# 3. Earth, Air, Fire, & Water

## Elements And Magick

*Fire, Fire, Earth, Earth.*
*Magick, Magick, come to birth.*
*Water, Water. Air, Air.*
*Magick, Magic, everywhere.*

Earth, Air, Fire, Water, Spirit - the five elements that make up life on this Earth that we live on. All life consists of them and their inherent energies and it is these energies that we use to make magic, along with our own energy or power, call it what you will.

So what is this magic and where does it come from? Natural magic uses the powers in and around us that we can all see and feel, the rushing of the waters, the wind in our hair, the flame of a candle, a flower in bloom, birth, growth and death. By using the energies of the elements or any other type of magic will not make your wishes materialise in front of you, but will create the necessary energies around you to attract the situation needed to fulfil your desire. An earth spell for money won't make a cheque fall onto your doormat, but it will attract the right energy and situations from where money will come, the chance of a promotion perhaps, or employment if your are currently unemployed. Natural magic is subtle, working with the natural flow of energies already in existence to bring about the necessary changes. It's not an instant fix, but you will be amazed at what can happen when you unleash the power around you.

Natural or elemental magick is neither wrong nor evil, nor is it supernatural coming as it does from nature itself. There is no devil or satanic being governing the laws of magic but simply a force that exists and that can be directed, similar to electricity and like electricity, magic requires a healthy respect otherwise you may get a nasty 'kick' from it. By working with it, in harmony with the Earth itself we set free valuable positive energies that return to nature and help to heal this planet that supports us and in today's global crisis that can be no bad thing, can it?

The Cottage Witch had no truck with musty old books of ceremonial magic or lengthy Latin or Hebrew prose, she used the herbs in her store cupboard or garden, the water from her well, discarded feathers, and the fire in her hearth. Natural magic uncluttered with years of study cloaking what she knew instinctively and how to use it was her way.


**Earth Magic**

This Element speaks for itself as the earth that we live on, that we grow our food in and on. The solid stable element that we can see and feel, earth is the element that we work with when we are casting spells for money, prosperity, matters of employment, financial security and for fertility or 'grounding' and physical safety. Garden magic and plant magic respond well to the earth element for obvious reasons. Earth is the nurturing element and it is to the earth that we return our dead.

Each element is associated with a particular colour or colours which can be used when choosing candles appropriate to the element, or material for spell bags, both of which are covered in greater detail in later chapters. The colour of the earth element is of course green or brown.

Along with specific colours, the elements have direct associations with particular tools and creatures known as elemental spirits or 'elementals'. In the case of earth, the pentacle or plate is the tool and the elementals of earth are the gnomes.

Herbs play an important part in earth magic with their direct association to the earth itself but as can be discovered later in the chapter Parsley, Sage, Rosemary and Thyme certain herbs have more influence on and from the earth element, especially those that actually smell of earth such as patchouli.

One of the best ways to relate to the element of earth is by the food we eat, especially root vegetables that actually grow beneath the surface of earth. The chapter Witchin' In The Kitchen gives some easy and fun ideas for casting spells as we cook or eat.

A quick and easy earth spell for keeping the kids safe when they are away from home is to keep a pot of earth by the door and as they leave for school or wherever, toss a pinch of earth after them, without them seeing or knowing, and mentally picture them returning happy and safe.

Burying an object that relates to your need, either in the garden or a plant pot, and visualising the desired outcome is also a quick but powerful earth spell that works. Need extra cash to pay an unexpected bill? Write 'PAID' in bold red letters across the bill, fold it up, bury it and 'see' it paid.

Planting a seed of an earth related herb or plant, basil for instance, telling it that as it grows, so do your finances is a spell that works.

All spells, no matter how simple and straightforward, require one thing to make them work, your energy and knowing that it will work. Have no doubt or the negative energy that you send out with the doubt will negate the spell.

## Air magic

Air, the element that keeps us alive, the air we breathe seen as the wind in the trees, leaves blowing over our gardens and in its forceful, destructive form as hurricanes and cyclone.

Air is the element in magic that governs thinking, knowledge, and intelligence. It helps spells for travel, for freedom, teaching and finding lost objects.

The colour associated with the element of air is yellow and the elemental creatures of air are called sylphs, which are winged, fairy-like creatures. The knife is the tool associated with air magic, as is the magic of incense smoke, divination, wind magic and visualisation.

Passing an object connected to your desire through fragrant incense smoke whilst mentally picturing the successful outcome is a simple air spell. For quicker results drop the object out of an upstairs window (place a cushion on the ground to protect the object if it's fragile!). Or draw a symbol that associates your thoughts with the problem or the desired object, crumple up the paper and toss it into the air, telling the air to energise your spell. Catch it, toss it, catch it, toss it visualising the air working its magic on the spell and then when you feel the air has done it's work place the spell onto a flame proof dish and burn it, releasing the energy of your spell into the air with the rising smoke. You are also using the power of the transforming fire element here, too.

To call the winds, stand outside and whistle whilst facing each direction in turn. 'See' the winds rising and 'feel' the wind ruffling your hair.

Tying a symbol of your desire to a kite or drawing a symbol onto the kite itself or one of the 'tails' and flying it in the wind whilst visualising the successful outcome is a simple way of using air energy, whilst combining your time with playing with the kids.

Feathers are a powerful symbol of air. If you wish to travel to a specific location , draw a simple map or write the name of the place you wish to visit, place a feather with it, tie it up in a yellow cloth and hang it on your washing line or the branch of a tree to blow about in the breeze. 'See' yourself at your destination and leave the air to do it's work.

**Fire magic**

Fire transforms and purifies all things, it changes the form of a substance either from a liquid to a gas (water into steam) a solid into a liquid (ice to water, solid candle wax into liquid) or from a dense solid into a more fragile substance (wood to ash). Fire magic governs all transformations, creative energies, and destructive ones. It is a cleansing energy and also relates to sexual energies. It can be invoked to induce protection, courage and strength or to get rid of negativity.

The candle flame and the cooking pot and of course the fireplace or the oven are all used in fire magic. You don't need the cauldron over the open fire that the cottage witch lived with; a pan over a gas flame or even on an electric hob will do the job too.

Hot, stimulating foods can be used in fire magic, like chilli peppers, ginger, or hot coffee, all a lot easier to get than the elaborate ingredients in some spells I have seen.

Burning and smouldering of symbolic objects or spells written on paper in conjunction with candles are excellent ways of employing fire magic. Red is the colour associated with the fire element and the elementals creatures are called salamanders.
The witch's knife, sometimes known as an athame (pronounced a-thay-me) is the tool of fire.

When using fire energy in spell work extra care and respect is naturally called for with open flames. Once when striking a match during a fire spell, I inadvertently struck the match towards me rather than away from me. The lit end of the match parted company with the remainder and as I was wearing a fairly low cut T-shirt at the time it headed straight down the front of my bra where it nestled hotly in my cleavage. This has gone down in history as the Rite of the Flaming Boobs. A cautionary tale that could have had a far more serious ending. I shall say no more!

Gazing into the flame of a candle or the flames of a fire can be a powerful aid to divination or the induction of psychic visions.


**Water magic**

The calming, cooling element of water governs all magick associated with emotions, love, happiness, absorption and germination of ideas. It is healing, purifying and cleansing.

Water magick can be performed in the obvious places like the seashore or lakeside, but don't forget the ever present source of water in our everyday lives, the sinks and taps in our kitchens and bathrooms. Bathwater spiked with the specific herb for your purpose combines an everyday necessity with spellworking. Purification energy is easily obtained by standing under a powerful jet of water from your morning shower, providing that whilst standing there you visualise the water cleansing and removing unwanted energy or illness and literally washing it away down the plughole!

A simple love spell is to inscribe the initial or name of your loved one onto a rose petal and toss it into a stream or river visualising the water carrying your love token to the object of your desire. It's okay to throw flowers into streams or rivers but it goes without saying that parchments or papers treated this way are a no no.

Mirrors come under the influence of water magick because of the their reflective cool appearance and their likeness to a placid lake surface.

Blue is the colour of the water element and the elemental creatures are mermaid-like beings called Undines.


## Spirit

Spirit, or Akashic energy as it is known is probably more easily understood if viewed as the container and creator of all of the other elemental energies, the Mother element if you like. It holds all other elemental energy in balance and all life is pervaded with it. Akashic energy is Earth and Spirit, Air and Spirit, Fire and Spirit, Water and Spirit. It is Akashic energy that feeds the intuition sparked by the Air element, and Akashic energy that gives life to the passion of Fire magick. And so it is for all magick, Akasha brings the feeling and meaning to all your magick and spell workings. Akasha is 'All'.

# 4. The Witch's Tools

*Time of trouble, Cauldron bubble.*
*Use the Broom, at Full of Moon.*
*Wand of fire, Man's desire.*
*Sacred Cup, With Gods I sup.*
*Power knife, Spell to life.*
*Magick flame in Goddess name.*
*Tools of power, moonlit hour.*
*Forest glade, magick made.*

Here we enter the territory of sacred objects or tools for carrying out simple ritual and spellcasting. Our cottage witch would have used the implements that she already had in her home, kitchen knives, the broom or besom that she cleaned her floors with and swept dirt and 'negativity' away. Her cauldron was her cooking pot over her open fire or range.

I am a firm advocate of DIY in this instance. If you can possibly create or adapt your own tools then they will be charged with your own energy and potential and will serve you well. You can if you wish buy them from the occult supply stores but the magick definitely begins with the creation of your working tools. There are some tools that you will, out of necessity purchase, unless you happen to be a metalsmith or potter, but these tools can be imbued with your own essence by decoration or adaptation of everyday objects. Some of the tools will come from Mother Nature herself and she will give them to you freely and with love, I do however believe that we should always ask permission before taking anything from nature. This can be done by silently contemplating the object, a straight branch of the hazel tree for instance, that you intend to fashion into your wand. Try to mentally reach out to the tree and ask if you may take the branch. If you feel positive and good about it, then I would say that permission has been granted. Negative feelings or the absence of any feeling would indicate that the tree would really rather keep that particular branch. Thank the tree and look elsewhere. Always leave a token of thanks for anything that you take from nature; a shiny coin, a silver button or a crystal, will always be welcomed by the earth spirits.

The witch's tools all relate to the elements. The wand is the tool of fire, the cup and cauldron relate to water and the plate or pentacle is the tool of the earth element. Candles work with the fire element and the knife is governed by air. Some of the tools overlap and are associated with more than one of the elements. The incense burner for example, relates to both air and fire. Burning herbs is transforming fire energy, but the resulting fragrant smoke comes under the influence of the element of air.

Don't worry or get into a panic about the tools, they will all become a part of you, your friends, and you will use them instinctively, working your magick like a veteran witch in no time.

### The ritual knife/herb knife

The ritual knife, the athame, is usually a double-edged blade with a black handle and is used solely for casting circles and other ritual use, which will be enlarged upon later. The herb knife, or bolline (pronounced bo-leen) has a white handle and is used for gathering herbs, wood for wands (it needs to be sharp!), carving candles and any other cutting activity associated with the 'craft.' Some witches do combine the two and quite successfully too but in the early stages I would recommend that you keep them separate.

Unless you happen to be a silver or coppersmith you are going to have to buy your knives, but your energies can be infused into their creation by purchasing plain, simple knives from any kitchenware store and engraving the handles with magickal symbols yourself. Not only will they be more powerful because of your part in their creation, they will also cost you a lot less.

These symbols can be carved with a craft knife, or burned into the handle using a hot needle, or simply painted on. Whichever method you decide on the symbols are entirely up to you, although I would suggest that somewhere on the handle is a pentagram and the symbol for the Goddess.

## The wand

This is the one tool that you can and should make yourself. The wand is associated with the element of fire and its function is that of transmitter, sending energy/personal power from you into a spell or object.

Traditionally, wands are cut from living wood of one year's growth and should measure from your elbow to your fingertips. Many believe that they should be cut at sunrise on Midsummer day, fine if you can, but if you have kids to get to school first this isn't an easy thing to do. I believe that it is far better to cut and fashion your own wand at a time when it is practical and suitable to you than to buy it or have someone else make it for you. Remember the cottage witch? She above all else was practical. If you happen to be restricted or attracted to a branch on a fallen tree then go for it. It has spoken to you for a reason. The power is your own personal energy and you will transmit that into the wand as you create it.

So which tree are you going to ask for your wand? Traditionally, wands are of oak, willow or hazel, but you could use a wood that is in harmony with your nature or the intent of a specific spell. My wand is of elder because it has long been associated with witches and fairies. Spirits of old witches are supposed to dwell within the branches of the elder, and even be able to transform themselves into an elder tree. There is enough folk-lore surrounding the elder to fill a chapter, but I will refrain at this time. A short table giving the associations to specific trees is to be found in the last chapter 'End Bits'.

Okay, you've found your tree and all is well, permission is given to take the wood, what now? The branch should be cut using the herb knife (I did say it had to be kept sharp!) and the chosen gift left in thanks for the wood.

The outer bark needs to be peeled away and this is usually easier whilst the wood is green. Once the wand is down to the bare wood it needs to be left to dry for a couple of days. At this stage you can begin to charge the wand. Hold it in both hands and feel your own energy flowing into the wand and think about what you will be using the wand for, 'see' yourself using it. If you intend to name your wand, it is at this time that its secret name may come to you. If it does, then name it right there and then but remember, the names given to your tools should be told to no-one.

If you have a permanent altar, leave your wand on it to charge for a few days. If not you could leave it on a windowsill where it will receive the energies of the sun and the moon. Once it is dry, sand it carefully to remove any sharp growing points and to make it smooth.

Carving symbols on the wand is an important step. Again, the symbols, if any, are up to you. Some witches like to embellish their wands with crystal points at the ends, bound tightly to the wand with copper wire, which also acts as an energy conductor. However you decide to personalise your wand, do it with visualisation and love.

Not every one of us is able or free to wander among woods or parks, what then? If you live in a town and have no access to a tree, then it's okay to call into the nearest DIY shop and purchase a small length of dowelling, remember, your energy is what is important here and carving or inscribing your symbols on it, charging it on your altar will impart your own magic into it.

There is always a way.

This may look like a lengthy process but it can be done over several days or weeks or months, it's up to you. The important thing at the end of the day is that your wand is truly a work of your own magic.

The wand is the male symbol and can be used in place of the knife to cast circles and bless wine etcetera.

## The cup

The cup is the symbol of the water element, of love and of the womb of the Goddess. It is the vessel from which ritual wine is blessed and drunk, a direct connection to the Goddess.

Unless you are a potter or have access to a potters wheel, the cup is another of the tools that you may have to purchase. It doesn't necessarily have to be a chalice emblazoned with a pentagram although there are some beautiful ones available. I personally think that a beautiful glass goblet that you have found in a department store, a car boot sale or charity shop, an ordinary wine glass, a ceramic drinking goblet, whatever 'speaks' to you as a ritual cup is best. In times past, the cup of the cottage witch was simply the best drinking vessel that she owned. It bore no ritual or religious markings for fear of persecution, but she would 'mark' the cup with a pentagram using her finger dipped into wine or water.

## The besom (broom)

The broom is a symbol of both Goddess and God. The handle of the broom represents the masculine and the twigs surrounding it form the feminine principle of the womb. The symbolism here speaks for itself I think!

Our cottage witch would sweep her home clean with her besom, and she would also sweep away unseen psychic debris that may be cluttering her space. People visiting can bring unwanted psychic energy, we can leave behind old energy from our completed spellworkings, in fact psychic debris can come from many sources. There is no need to be paranoid about this, it happens and we can get rid of it by ritually sweeping it away with our broom or besom that has been created or charged for this purpose. I don't mean that you should get the broom out every time visitors leave but on a regular basis when you do your everyday cleaning. The broom is also used to cleanse the sacred area or circle before working, but I will discuss this in the chapter 'Sacred Space'.

Store your besom above or behind the front door of your home, it will act as a guardian of the doorway, and be there ready to sweep away any negative energy. If you can make your broom then do so, but if not buy a new broom and keep it solely for this purpose, cleaning out the coal shed with it may just take the edge of its power! Making it is simple, gather twigs, preferably of hazel and bind them around a stout branch using strong garden twine topped with red ribbon. Always remember to ask the necessary permissions from the tree spirits involved in your choice of twigs and wood.

## The cauldron

No self-respecting witch can be seen without a cauldron, just look at all the fairy-story books and the ornaments in the gift shops! In fact the cauldron will probably become the tool that you use the most. No, it doesn't have to be made of cast iron and you don't have to build a fire in the middle of your living room (it will just make a mess of the carpet) but it should be a heavy-duty cooking pot that you will use only for spellworking and all those lovely magick potions. You don't need to spend a fortune, scout around the car boot sales and the discount shops, you may already have a large pan that you can use. The pot doesn't need to be heavy in itself but it should have a heavy base, it's going to be getting a lot of use. The colour is up to you and of course you can paint your magick symbols on the outside (high up if you are going to put it on the open flame of a gas ring!).

The cauldron represents the element of water, like the cup, and is symbolic of the womb of the Goddess, perfect for creating magick. It is also a symbol of Akasha or Spirit as the symbol of pure creation.

## The plate (pentacle)

The plate or pentacle is the symbol of the earth element. It is usually of wood or clay and is a round disc or plate, traditionally marked with a pentagram and optionally other symbols (Goddess or Earth symbols). It is used on the altar for the placement of ritual offerings or the placement of spells etc.

A handsome pentacle can be made using the modelling clay that hardens on its own which is freely available and inexpensive. Simply roll it out like pastry, cut it into a round and inscribe it as you wish. I have seen one constructed this way with the addition of a few polished gemstones of amethyst and rose quartz around the edge. Made by that witch's own fair hands it held pride of place on her altar, and rightly so, it was very beautiful. A sawmill would be able to provide you with a slice of wood quite cheaply but you would have to allow this to season before carving it or painting the symbols on it. You may even draw the pentacle on paper if you wish.

Alternatively you may have a plain plate already in your cupboard which you can decorate yourself with the appropriate symbols.

**Witch's journal (book of shadows)**

You will want to document your workings and rituals. Whether you use the ones contained in this book, others, or write your own (which I hope you do eventually) your journal will be a permanent record of all your 'witcheries'. This can be anything from a humble notebook, a loose-leaf binder to a leather bound work of art. Whatever the format, it is important to record your spells, recipes and rituals. At a later date when you want to repeat a spell, everything is there at your fingertips.

In times past a witch's Book of Shadows was buried or burned with her on her passing so important and personal to her was it.

If you start with a notebook for instance, choose a plain covered one and then you can adorn it yourself with pentagrams, Goddess symbols etcetera. You will find over the years that your Book of Shadows will evolve with you and if the time comes that you wish to copy your work into a new Book I would recommend that the original is burned after you have taken from it all that you feel relevant.

## Other bits'n'bobs

*Pestle and Mortar*
The magickal energies that live within the wonderful herbs that can be easily grown at our own kitchen door, on a windowsill or purchased at the local supermarket, begin their transformation and release when we grind them in the pestle and mortar. These are ground to a fine powder or larger granules depending on what we intend to do with them. Our magickal intention begins to become focused on the spell at this point. The pestle and mortar are also obvious symbols of the male and female divine essences, bringing the Goddess and God energies into our magickal workings. In today's kitchen the pestle and mortar are replaced by the food processor or electric coffee grinder. Whilst these are not as romantic as the pestle and mortar, they are every bit as effective and very practical. If you have ever spent hours trying to reduce cedar wood shavings to the smallest possible component of incense you will know what I mean! Fine if you have the time, but I'm guessing that because you are reading this book, time is not your friend right now. Does it still work? Of course. Once the processor or grinder has reduced the ingredients to the size required, then your magickal focus can flower, as you enchant the herbs to the spell. More on that in Hocus Pocus and Eye of Newt.

*Incense burner*
You will need a sturdy bowl in which to burn incense. It can be any pretty ceramic bowl, or brass or other metal bowl. One that you already have or one you find on that interesting stall at the boot sale will be perfect. You will need to fill it half way up with soil or sand otherwise the heat from the burning charcoal will be transferred to the altar or table making a nasty mark on your piece of furniture and speaking from experience charcoal blocks come to life when lit. There was an occasion when celebrating the autumn equinox ..... remember the altar fire? Yep, the glowing charcoal sputtered, broke in

half, hit the altar cloth which then caught fire and the rest as they say, is history. It wasn't even a fire festival! (See Seasons and Celebrations).

*Altar cloths*

These are optional. My own household altar is a lovely old dresser and I can't bring myself to cover it up but if you wish to use altar cloths, you can find some lovely shawls and scarves in charity shops, boot sales or markets. If you are handy with a needle then by all means stitch some of your own magic into the cloth of your choice. One witch that I know bought some sari material which was quite beautiful and as it was a fairly small piece she bought it for next to nothing, it always looks stunning.

If you choose to have an altar cloth then you may wish to ring the changes with the season with regards to colour. I will talk about this in more detail in the chapter Seasons and Celebrations.

*Jewellery*

Traditionally, witches wear a necklace. This can be of any type, crystal chips, beads or even a simple chain. It is the symbolism of the circle of life that is important, reminding us of the ever-spinning wheel of birth, death and rebirth. If you wish to wear a necklace that you dedicate to your workings, choose one that has meaning for you.

*Ritual Robes/Clothing*

This is an old chestnut that causes a difference of opinion amongst many witches. I will continue to harp on the recurring theme here, 'whatever rings true to you'. You may find it difficult, uncomfortable or inconvenient to change into a ritual robe before every spellcasting or simple rite. You may wish to wear a ritual robe on special celebrations only but bear this in mind, our friend the cottage witch, who performed her powerful magic and worshiped the Goddess on a daily basis would not have had any ritual robes and in the British climate, I guess she would have considered anyone mad that jaunted around the countryside in their birthday suit. There was no gloss on her 'Craft', she was simply all that she was. The Goddess knows what is underneath a ritual robe anyway and can see into the true heart whether the ritual is done in a robe or a pair of jeans.

*Candles and Herbs*
Spell working and ritual use of both candles and herbs are detailed in the chapters Parsley, Sage, Rosemary and Thyme and Candle, Candle Burning Bright but they should be mentioned here as they are indeed important tools of the witch.

The herbs that are featured can all be found either already in your store cupboard or in your local shop or supermarket. Whilst there are hundreds of books detailing the ritual use of every known herb or spice known to man, we are interested here only in what is readily available. The witch of old would have no access to Dragon's Blood and the like, but Parsley and other humble herbs would be put to very good and effective use.

If you are lucky enough to have a garden, however small, try growing a few herbs. Not only will they enhance your garden and attract the fairy folk into it, using herbs that you have grown and tended with your own hands must be the best way of using them. If you have no garden what about a window box? Or a pot on the windowsill?

The flame of a candle has it's own beauty but when used as part of a spell or ritual it becomes a powerful source of magick. The use of candles in magick is one of the most ancient of practices and with so many beautifully coloured or decorated candles available now at reasonable cost the possibilities are endless. If you wish to make your own

candles, then that too is simple and packed with an energy that is all yours.

## Consecration of your tools

Okay, you have your tools, now it's time to make them sacred, dedicated to you and your Craft. I have included a simple Rite of Consecration in Rites and Rituals but feel that this chapter is incomplete without discussing this necessary part of the creation or gathering together of your tools.

It is important that the tools that you are using, even though they were perhaps once in general use in your household, should now only be used for spell working or ritual and they shouldn't be used by anyone else. This way your own power will increase constantly in the tools as you use them and be uncluttered with everyday energy. If you wish to name any of your tools and haven't already done so, then this can be done during the rite of consecration.

So now you're ready to get to work. Happy witching.

# 5. The Witch's Altar and Sacred Space

*Sacred table of burnished wood*
*In magick circle cast for good*
*To honour the God and Goddess of Old*
*Enchantment and spells worth more than gold*
*Polished and loved, kept shining with care*
*Stand you before it and know They are there*
*Candles alight and scented smoke curling*
*By Earth, Air and Fire, magick is swirling*

Why an altar? Where should it be and what should be on it?

In all religions there is a focal point for the performing of ritual or ceremony. It is dedicated to the Goddess or God of that religion whether pagan or otherwise. They are places of communion between the worlds, where we can 'meet' with the Goddess or God and/or carry out spell working or ritual.

A witch's altar can be anything from a coffee table to a tree stump. Whatever you choose to consecrate and use as your altar will be a personal thing and will also depend on space and a hoard of other considerations. Does your partner object to a traditional altar? Will you fall over it if it is left in place permanently? Do you want an indoor altar or a fallen tree in a wood?

You can choose to have just one altar or a main 'household' altar and several 'satellite' altars, in the kitchen, the bedroom, the garden, a local park, or woodland clearing.

42

Whatever you choose, it should be dedicated or consecrated whether it be a permanent altar or your coffee table.

A friend of mine chose a windowsill for her altar as her partner was uncomfortable with the traditional look. There is always a vase of fresh flowers or greenery sitting on her pentacle between two candles. She has a stick incense ash catcher and a pretty ceramic goblet arranged there too. These blend together in her own mind to form her altar, and her husband just thinks it looks pretty. The important thing is, to her, it is sacred space.

I have a main household altar in my living room and another in the kitchen, housed in a quiet corner, in an old stone bread oven that we found whilst 'unmodernising' our cottage.

I have also seen an altar on a bird table in a garden. That particular witch has a strong psychic link to all bird life and is very rarely to be found indoors. She painted a pentagram on the base of the table and arranged two garden flares at either side. A stone wine cup is always filled with fresh spring water that her feathered friends are always delighted to share with her.

The possibilities are endless and you don't have to construct a stereotypical altar to create your own sacred space. Set your imagination free and make your altar your own.

What should be on your altar? Your working tools, the cup, plate, and knife should have a prominent place there, along with symbols of the Goddess and God. These can be anything as simple as a pair of candles to a sculpture or carving. There are many beautiful statues of the Goddess to be found, but whilst they are beautiful they are not essential. A round and a long stone or crystal, or a picture can represent the Goddess and God, or if your altar is close to a window where the moonlight and sunlight can touch it what can be better that?

A heavy based bowl half filled with earth or sand in which to burn incense is the last of the essentials. The rest is up to you, make it as uncomplicated or elaborate as you like.

I hope that you are beginning to see how simple everything to do with cottage witchcraft is. It is a basic expression of your beliefs and energies with no frills and a no nonsense way of living your 'Craft'.

Sacred space is simply the environment that is suitable for making magick and communicating with the Goddess and God. Much has been said and written about the creation of magick circles ranging from painting a circle directly onto the floor to marking it out with tape etcetera, prior to casting the circle. Its purpose is to protect the witch and her working from negative outside influences, and I don't mean the boogey man. It is also to contain the power or energy that is raised during the spell casting, enabling it to build up to a crescendo, giving it extra oomph when it is released. In reality, at the end of a busy day or when you are snatching five minutes whilst the baby is sleeping this isn't going to happen.

Will it affect your magic? No.

The magick comes from within you and is poured out during the act of casting a spell. This is going to happen whether or not you are standing inside a magick circle. The energy will dissipate slightly but when all is said and done it is far better to carry out spell working without the circle than not at all. How can we get over this?

The magick circle is constructed astrally, that is, you create it by directing your own energy outward in a circle and 'seeing' the energy forming a protective circle or barrier around you. 'Must I do this every time I want to do a little spell, or light a healing candle for a sick friend?' I hear you ask. No, of course not. What I would suggest is that you create your astral fortress not as a circle within the room that you are working, but encompassing your whole home. This can be repeated at intervals when you feel the energy needs replenishing.

You can of course cast your circle for rituals within the room or area that you are working if you wish, especially if you are working outside and the way to do this is included in Rites and Rituals.

# 6. Seasons and Celebrations

*Spring, Summer, Winter and Fall*
*Hearken to Our Lady's call*
*Wind and rain, sun and snow*
*Cycles and tides begin to flow*
*She loves and weds, gives us her son*
*At Yuletide when the year's begun*
*Solstice, Moon and Sabbat night*
*The wheel turns on beyond our sight.*

The witch's year can be likened to a wheel with its spokes representing the cycles of the lives of the Goddess and God, cleverly intertwined with the changing seasons. As the wheel turns we celebrate accordingly.

There are eight annual celebrations in the witch's year; four fire festivals that trace the cycles of the Goddess and four solar festivals relating to the life and death of the God. These are viewed by some as major and minor celebrations or sabbats, with the fire festivals dominating. If we are to look for balance though, I feel that the solar or God festivals should share importance in the year with those of the Goddess.

In addition to the annual celebrations there are the milestones or rites of passage that we mark with ritual. These are birth, with the wiccanning, marriage or handfasting and death with the celebration we call requiem.

The Mother Goddess is also acknowledged in ritual at the full moons, thirteen in the year.

It is important both psychologically and spiritually for the witch to celebrate all of these occasions and mark the turning of the wheel with her/his own ritual. So, in keeping with the spirit of the cottage witch, the rituals that follow for each of these are simple and straightforward. Of course, as always, these rituals are just the signposts that point the way, make your own detours or find your own path if you can. The results will be very satisfying and much more powerful than reciting the words of someone else.

The fire festivals mark the beginning of each season, they are Imbolc (meaning 'in the belly') on February 2nd, Beltane on April 31st or May Eve, Lammas on July 31st or August Eve, and Samhain ( pronounced sow-en) on October 31st.

The solar or God festivals fall on the solstices and equinoxes and mark the mid point of the seasons. Yule or the Winter Solstice falls on Dec 21st, Ostara or Spring Equinox on March 21st, Litha or Summer Solstice on June 21st (Midsummer Day) and Mabon, the Autumnal Equinox falls on Sept 21st. In reality, with the annual movement of planets and times and tides, these festivals do shift by a day or so from year to year, but then so do our birthdays, anniversaries and other important dates but we celebrate them on the same day each year. This gives structure to our celebrations and helps fix the changing of the seasons better in our psyche.

What can be seen from this is the overlapping of the Christian calendar at or around these dates, with Christmas, the birth of the Christian Sun God, their Child of Promise falling around Yule, Easter at Ostara, Candlemas at Imbolc and the Harvest Festivals fall on or around Lammas. Samhain or All Hallows (Halloween) is the time we remember those that we have known or loved who have passed over, it is a time of

48

endings and beginnings and before the introduction of our present calender it was celebrated as the New Year.

At this point it is perhaps appropriate to mention the timing of these celebrations. You may read from other books and hear from other witches that they celebrate these times on the nearest convenient day, usually the nearest Saturday. This is probably because they are coven witches and the weekend is the best time for gathering all together. Now, whilst I have advocated meandering from the signed road, I do believe that these times and tides should be marked on the right dates. This is necessary If we are to stay in tune with the tides of nature and certainly the full moons should be marked accordingly, given that the moon is full for three nights each time, so there are three opportunities to acknowledge her. Remember, the ways of the cottage witch are simple and can be as uncomplicated as lighting a candle, the important thing is that we recognise and feel the movements of the seasons and cycles of our lives on this Earth. There, that is the one and only time that you will hear me be dogmatic about the Craft!

Suggested rituals for all of these festivals are included in Rites and Rituals.

## Yule – December 21st

As Yule is almost upon us as I write this it is perhaps appropriate that this is the first Sabbat we look at in detail, it is also the first festival of the pagan year. The Sun God, the Child of Promise, is reborn at Yule. Born of the Mother to grow into manhood, he will bring light and life to the earth, eventually to be sacrificed at Lammas and reborn at Yule. And so the wheel turns. Yule falls between 17th and 25th December and is traditionally celebrated on 21st.

Many of the traditions of Christmas are simply carried on from the pagan activities at Yule. The Christmas tree, the bringing in of evergreens into the home was a symbol of the continuance of life in the depths of winter and the twinkling lights we see in all the windows and on trees everywhere were candles in past times. Lights to show the Sun God the way back to the Earth, to encourage his light to shine once more. Tinsel and glittery party dresses all perpetuate the bringing back of the light and we give of our own light by visiting and entertaining friends during this season of goodwill.

Yule is the season of joy and of new beginnings, even the tradition of giving gifts at Christmas comes from the days when people would give gifts to mark the birth of the Child of Promise, birthday presents!

For the witch, Yule is a time for the stirring of ideas and creativity, the formulating of goals and projects that you wish to accomplish in the coming year, the time to think about new employment if you are unhappy in your present job or maybe to look at the starting of a new hobby or pastime.

Although it is traditional for the tree to be brought into the home and decorated at Yule, it is nothing unusual to see trees and lights in windows as early as the end of November. This practice may be fine for the non-witch but ask yourself how we can stay in tune with nature's cycles and the seasonal celebrations when we begin them as much as a month early! I know it is difficult when there are small children in the home, their friends have twinkly, magickal trees in their living room and the shops and streets are crowded with festive decorations and of course they want their tree and the decorations up as soon as you are willing, or they manage to drive you crazy until you comply. Been there and done that!

The way I used to get around it was to put the tree and evergreen decorations up around the second week in

December but leave the topping off of the tree until Yule, then the fairy (the representative of the Goddess and the Otherworld), or five-pointed star was placed reverently on the top and everyone was happy. We have to live in today's world and amongst friends and loved ones who do not always share our views and beliefs, finding a happy middle ground seems the best way to remain at peace with others and ourselves without compromising the core of our beliefs.

The Goddess leaves us at Yule in her dark Goddess phase on her journey to the underworld to return at Imbolc as the Maiden but she keeps her vigil over the Earth and her children.

Your altar decorations at Yule should include evergreens, red ribbons and red candles. It can be as simple or elaborate as you wish. If you use an altar cloth choose from red, gold or dark green.

Incense for Yule should include any from the following: Bay, Frankincense, Myrrh, Cinnamon and Orange.

## Imbolc – February 2nd

Imbolc is the first of the annual fire festivals and beacon fires were lit on hilltops. The Goddess returns to us from the Underworld at Imbolc in her phase as the Maiden. Imbolc means 'in the belly' and life is felt stirring in the womb of the Mother. It is sometimes known as the Festival of Lights as candles are lit throughout the home encouraging the Sun to gather in strength with each new dawn. Imbolc is about light and life overcoming the darkness and sterility of the winter.

It is the time of gestation. Of putting into motion any plans or ideas that first stirred in your imagination at Yule, a time of purification ready for the birth of this new creativity.

It is at Imbolc that we see the first stirring or promise of Spring. It is still cold and in some parts snow and frosts still cover the ground, there are still no leaves on the trees but if we look carefully, the fragile white heads of the snowdrops can be seen poking above the frozen earth. A folk name for the snowdrop is Candlemas Maiden, so faithful are they in their appearance at this time. My grandmother used to call them the 'Brave Snowdrops' as they appeared in all their beauty at the coldest and harshest time to show us that Spring is just around the corner and the wheel is still turning quietly out of our sight.

Plant seeds in pots to represent your goals and ambitions and watch them grow, knowing that as the seeds sprout and grow stronger and eventually reach maturity, so will your plans and wishes. Remember though that just as plants need nurturing with food and water so do our plans. We can't expect a healthy plant to grow with no attention, so nurture your wishes with any necessary actions.

Your Imbolc altar should include white candles, snowdrops if you can find them, and the altar cloth should be white.

Imbolc incense might include Frankincense, the first flower available where you live, a drop or two of red wine, basil.


**Ostara – 21st March**

Spring's promise is fulfiled at Ostara, the Spring Equinox. Everywhere the Goddess is bursting forth in leaf, bud and stem. Trees are beginning to leaf, spring flowers are seen in gardens, parks and hedgerows and lambs are wobbling around on newborn legs. Ostara is about fertility and purification and named after the Spring Goddess Eostre (Easter).

Spring cleaning the home, getting rid of unwanted dust and clutter from cupboards and closets, ridding ourselves or any unwanted psychic or mental clutter are all begun on the Spring Equinox. This too is the origin of the tradition of Easter Eggs and Easter Bunnies. Whilst the Easter Eggs were not of chocolate in the times of our cottage witch, the first eggs of Ostara would be decorated and placed on altars and tables as symbols of new life. March Hares have, over time, merged with the fertility association of rabbits, and Easter Bunnies and Easter Chicks all perpetuate the theme of fertility at this time.

The Spring Equinox also marks a time of balance. The hours of light and darkness are equal now and afterwards the hours of daylight begin to lengthen. All magicks concerning balance are fortunate at this time along with those of banishing negativity and increasing fertility and material needs.

Ostrara altars may be decorated with yellow candles, spring flowers, painted eggs and babies bootees. The altar cloth, if you use one, should be yellow.


**Beltane – April 30th (May eve)**

Beltane means Bel Fire after the Celtic God Belenius. It is a fire festival marking the God winning the hand of the Goddess. He has grown to maturity and wooed the Lady and finally won her hand. The two are wed at Beltane. May Eve weddings are said to be particularly favoured by the Goddess for this reason. Nice to share a wedding anniversary with Her!

She transforms from Maiden to Mother at this time and fertility, desires and union are the themes. The Maypole is an obvious symbol of this union. In times gone by, and still today in remote rural areas, men and women went into the woods on Beltane and made love. Sharing in the union of the Goddess and God ensuring fertility to the land, their animals and to themselves. This was a time when under-population was a problem and not the reverse as it is today. It was one of the ways that they would ensure children would be born at the end of the year, giving mothers time to nurture and wean the babies before they would once again start working on the land alongside their husbands. Survival of all life being the keynote here, Beltane is an appropriate time to work magick for the survival of the human race, not because of under-population, but because of the damage that we wreak on a daily basis to ourselves and to our Mother.

At Yule we first gave energy to new projects and ideas that were then seeded at Imbolc. We were cleansed at Ostara in preparation for all this activity and now at Beltane, the time has come to give life to this creativity and to actively seek out our goals and ambitions.

The Green Man is amongst us at Beltane. He is the God of the growing crops and will watch over them until they are finally harvested.

Your Beltane altar could be decorated with white gauze (a symbol of the Goddesses bridal veil), your own wedding picture if you are married, any wild or garden flowers around your area at this time, red or silver candles. Any altar cloths should be silver or red. Incense may include Frankincense, rose petals, cowslips or marigold.


## Litha - June 21st (summer solstice )

Summer Solstice, the longest day. The Sun God is at the height of his powers now and soon the warmth and light will begin to wane. And the wheel turns on. It is a time for thanksgiving to the Sun God and preparation for the harvest before the dark days of winter will once again be upon us. It is a time of potency and full strength, when we must seize opportunities that may arise. Crops are high and energies are at a peak and can be put to good use for workings that tackle problems that have seemed without solution. The light is at its peak and Litha is a time for us to take our own light out there, to family, friends and any that we know that are in need of light.

Litha magick includes workings for success and achievement, potency and culmination. Remember those seeds of Imbolc and Beltane? Now is the time that they should have reached their maturity, nurture them knowing that soon they will be ready for harvest.

Altars at Litha should abound with summer flowers and fruit, oak boughs or oak leaves. Candles should be gold or orange or bright yellow. Litha incense should incorporate Frankincense, Rosemary, Thyme, Camomile and Rose.


**Lammas – August 1st**

Lammas is the harvest time, the corn is high and ripe and ready for cutting down. The God is sacrificed at this time, cut down by the hand of the Goddess, his blood will feed the Earth ensuring that the fields remain fertile and the crops will come again. The folk song John Barleycorn tells of his sacrifice. This theme is by no means unique to the Old Religion, the sacrificial God is seen in many disguises throughout all religions. In Christianity didn't the Son of God (The Sun God) allow himself to be cut down for the sake of the survival of man?

Sometimes called Lughnasagh, after the Sun God Lugh, Lammas is a time for thanksgiving for all the bounties of the Mother Earth and coincides with the Christian Harvest

Festivals. The first loaf baked from the harvest was called the Lammas Loaf and those that partook of it were particularly blessed. Not many of us bake our own bread today with busy lives and the convenience of readily available bread from bakeries and supermarkets, but Lammas is the time to have a go. If you don't have the time or energy, maybe at least buy a part baked loaf, pop it into the oven and let the smell of the baking bread fill your home, your heart and your soul. It is a reminder of the bounties of the Earth Mother and becomes central to the Lammas celebrations.

The Lammas altar is my favourite. If you can possibly obtain some ears of wheat then they should adorn the Lammas altar in a dominant position. Loaves of bread of varying shapes and sizes, fruit and vegetables and vine leaves (these can often be obtained from a friendly family member or neighbour who has a vine in their greenhouse, or purchased quite cheaply from a florist), and a bottle of country wine, some of which should be in your ritual cup. Candles should be orange or cream, and altar candles cream or pale yellow. This is one time that your white handled knife should be prominently placed on your altar to represent the sacrifice of the God at this time, for surely every herb or root that we cut with it, sacrifices a part of its life for our art. Lammas altar cloths are of gold or yellow.

## Mabon – September 21st (autumn equinox)

Once again the light and darkness are in balance. The nights begin to draw in on us after this festival and darkness once more conquers light. We sense the approach of winter and cold north winds are not far away. Also called the Second Harvest, it is a time of maximum abundance when we reap the bounty of the harvest, we reap what we have sown in a physical and spiritual sense and now we prepare to celebrate the waning of the year and the approach of the winter rest, for without winter there can be no new spring. Any of our dreams and wishes, goals or ambitions that have not been brought to fruition must be ploughed under for another year, for the next seedtime.

Mabon altars are always dressed in blues and green, for the cooling autumn rain and the green of the earth Mother. Flowers and candles should be chosen from amongst these shades. Altar cloths should be of a cool blue or a bright verdant green. Mabon incense may include a pulverised oak leaf, Frankincense, nuts and berries and bramble.

## Samhain – October 31st (Halloween)

Witches, ghoulies, ghosts and goblins are what we are led to believe Samhain is all about. In a way it's true, the veil between this world and the world of spirit is at its thinnest on this night and communion between the two is more likely. It is for remembering those that have passed on, not in a sad or grieving way but as a celebration of their lives that they have shared with us, and a time when we can invite them back into our homes for this fleeting of times.

The Goddess leaves us now to spend time in the Underworld as Persephone, but will return to us renewed at Imbolc. In this way She shows us that life is a continual cycle, the eternal return.

All Hallows Eve marks the beginning of the Celtic year so this is a dual celebration of endings and beginnings. By now the ever changing, ever present pattern of the eternal cycle of birth, death and rebirth or growth, maturity, rest and renewal, can be seen and felt.
Halloween's reputation of a night of evil comes from the belief in the fact that the dead can return at this time, and not everyone was welcome! It is a time of transition between the

years and it was believed that evil was abroad. The year is approaching it's death and energies are declining, all around can be felt the shift in the energies and the ascendance of the darkness. It was a time of unease and a time when faith in the rebirth of the Sun God and the return of the Goddess to her land was at it's strongest.

Cattle and pork were slaughtered and salted for meat for the coming winter and feasts on this night were traditional. Fires were lit to drive away bad spirits and the Jack O Lantern placed at the door for the same purpose. Although the pumpkin is an American import, country folk carved the Jack O Lanterns from suede or turnips.

Magick worked on Samhain should focus on rest before renewal, ageing and wisdom.

The Samhain altar is usually decorated with pumpkins, some of which can be carved as Jack O Lanterns, apples, ripe fruit and fallen leaves. Photographs or symbols of loved ones who have passed over may feature here as we welcome them back for this short period remembering happy times. Colours are the colours of fall, and dark midnight blues. Chrysanthemums are the flower of Samhain, they are the flower of the dead. Candles may be dark blue or black and the altar cloth of the same hue.

Incense at Samhain should include Chrysanthemum petals, Frankincense, pomegranate seeds.

**Yule – December 21st**

And so the wheel turns.

# 7. Ethics of the Craft and the Law of Return

*Magick spells and candle burning,*
*What goes out is soon returning.*
*Three times three the legend tells,*
*Be careful with your magick spells.*
*What you send comes back threefold,*
*The curse or charm will soon enfold*
*You in its power for good or bane,*
*From curse or hex you should refrain.*
*Send out light with love and care,*
*To know, to hush, to will, to dare.*
*'And it hurt none', the witch's charm,*
*Release the power but do no harm.*

Boomerang time! Whilst there are no rules or liturgies, or laws carved on tablets of stone, there are unwritten laws governing the use of magick and the Craft. It's not just a goody two-shoes attitude, it makes sound sense when you understand that the old saying 'what you sow, so shall you reap', is not just scare mongering or an attempt to coerce the practitioner into good behaviour, it is a fact. It is known as The Law of Rebound, The Law of Three Times Three, or The Threefold Law.

However you slice it, the truth is that whatever energies we use and release in the making of magick, be absolutely certain that you will soon be receiving a dose of the same. That being so it pays to avoid any use of harmful herbs, sending out of so-called curses (they don't work anyway so don't waste your time!), releasing negative energy, or deliberately causing harm, either mental or physical to another person.

This doesn't mean that we should lie down and take it on the chin when someone has a go at us, or does harm in any way to a friend or someone we love. No Siree. What we don't do is return like for like, thereby increasing the harmful energy that's floating around the place. It becomes a self-perpetuating yukky snowball that sooner or later is going to smack someone in the face. Let it not be you.

I know a woman that likes to call herself 'witch' who spends most of her time sending out negative energy to her neighbours (she actually calls it cursing) for various reasons, who then wonders why her own life is a shambles.

We can protect ourselves in many different ways, some of which I will explain in greater detail in the chapter Hocus Pocus and Eye of Newt but if you are absolutely sure that you are in need of protection from negative energy, an effective and permissible way of dealing with it is simply to reflect it back on the sender. That way they harm themselves (boomerang!) and you have consciously done no harm. Do this by placing a piece of mirror facing outwards on your window, facing the direction that you believe the harm to be coming from.

A word of caution here. It can be easy to convince yourself that you are the target of negative energy, so please don't allow yourself to become paranoid once working with magickal energy. Sometimes 'bad stuff' just happens. No-one does it, no-one sends it, no-one is to blame, it just happens. Be very certain that you actually need protection before invoking it or you could soon lose focus on what this is all about. A nervous wreck, for no reason, is of no use to anyone.

If you know that someone is causing you harm, magickally or otherwise, then the way to deal with it is to turn the energy around from negative to positive. Send love to them, send understanding (I know it's hard, I never said it was easy!), try to invent ways of making them see what they are doing, or simply walk away and forget it (harder still!).

When you are competent at spell casting, and it won't be long, you will find yourself working for others on a regular basis. Please don't be tempted to take payment for this. Remember that the energy that we use comes from inside us, it hasn't cost us anything, it is renewable, bio-degradable, environmentally friendly and free. Having said that, oils and herbs, or candles and cloth may have been purchased solely for the purpose of the spell working. By all means take payment for these items, but leave it at that. Remember, 'What you send comes back threefold', you will be paid in unexpected ways.

Finally, I would advise you to be modest about your Craft, people that really need you will find their path to your door anyway and you don't have to put an ad in the local rag or the Yellow Pages. The one thing that will be certain to trip you up is an enlarged ego. Magick is a gift, it isn't ours to buy or sell, and it won't fix everything, every time.

Wow, what a lot of Don'ts or so it seems. Here are a few Do's. Do love your Craft, Do stay close to nature, Do believe in magick and in yourself, Do unto others ... you know the rest, and lastly, Do have fun.

# Part Two

# Getting Down To It

# 8. Rites and Rituals

*Solstice, Sabbat and Full of Moon*
*Protection, Healing, or Ask a boon*
*Rites of Passage or casting spell*
*Ancient secrets none can tell*
*All within the circle round*
*Rites and rituals abound.*

The dictionary defines 'rites' as a ceremonial form or observance, and 'rituals' as the performance of rites. The Craft of the Witch is diverse and can be divided into religious observance and magickal spellcraft. All come under the term 'rites'. As can be seen in Seasons and Celebrations, observance is carried out on the eight major festivals and the full of the moon, Sabbats and Esbats. These rites are carried out within sacred space or a magick circle. This can be 'drawn' on every occasion but when your time is limited to a few precious minutes between crying babies and the washing up, for practical reasons, a 'super-circle' can be created around the entire home. When time is looking at you more kindly, then by all means draw or invoke your sacred space around the area that you will be working in.

For instance, the super-circle will be there constantly, allowing your entire home to be sacred space, this allows you to create spells in your kitchen as you cook your daily meals, take a ritual bath before bed or early in the morning and create magickal objects in your armchair in front of the TV, or place spells on your altar without the need for casting a circle each and every time. The super-circle can be 're-enforced' at intervals.

Of course, sacred space can be created at any time by casting a magick circle within the working area.

Why cast a circle when performing rites or casting spells? To create an area that will contain energy and personal power until it is released and to prevent unwanted or un-useable energy from entering your working area.

Your circle is cast by sending out your own personal power whilst visualising the energy creating an invisible sphere around you. The sphere is bisected by the floor, so that around and above you is a dome of energy. Some witches visualise the energy as a blue light coming from their fingers or working knives as they create this. The 'circle' is strengthened at the compass points by the relevant elemental energies, Air in the East, Fire in the South, Water in the West and Earth in the North and the presence of the Goddess and God.

If you pick up any number of books on the Craft, I'm sure you will find the circle casting ritual to contain references to 'summoning, calling or invoking' these energies and deities. Hm, I personally believe it to be impolite to address these beings in this way, and prefer to 'invite' them into my sacred space. I doubt if they would respond to 'summoning' if they didn't wish to anyway. Also, at the end of a ritual the circle is 'pulled' back in and these beings 'dismissed'. Again, I'm not happy with the idea of 'dismissing' deities and elemental energies. Impolite? Yes. Possible? Unlikely. And why would you want to send away these beautiful energies anyway? This is once again, another example of where Cottage Witchcraft and the more traditional and structured 'Craft' differ. I'm certain our friend in her cottage would never entertain the idea of 'shooing away' the Goddess after she has put in an appearance for her benefit.

Once the rite or ritual is ended and your consciousness moves on, the deities and elementals will lose interest any way and slowly dissipate of their own accord.

Your altar will be the pivotal point of any rite or ritual, be it an antique dresser, or the kitchen table and it is important to prepare your altar according to the occasion. This can be as elaborate or simple as you wish, be creative and use your ritual objects in a way that means something to you. I know I have said this before, but it really is important. Meaningless symbols and decorations may just as well be discarded for the value that they hold. You may have a beautiful sculpture of the Goddess, but if it's a rounded crystal, or holed stone that speaks to you with her voice, then, no contest. Similarly, if the beautiful sculpture warms you deep inside, makes you 'see' and feel Her, then it should have pride of place. I cannot emphasise enough, that in Cottage Witchraft, the use of what you have around you, that gives your ritual meaning and sparkle, is true magick.

I think it is appropriate here to discuss the human psyche in very brief detail. Our subconscious mind, the part of us that comes into play in trance, dream states, worship and the making of magick, responds to the language of pictures, symbols and verbally, to simple rhyme repeated over and over. How many nursery rhymes can you remember? How many pieces of prose? See what I mean? Simple, repetitive rhyme, chanted over and over become the spell, and because they activate our subconscious mind they are effective in magick. It doesn't matter how simplistic the rhyme is, the easier, the better. It follows then, that the Cottage Witch would en-'chant' her herbs, her spells and her potions and perform her rites and rituals in simple rhyme. You don't have to be Poet Laureate, or the inestimable Mr. Shakespeare, simple rhyme that you conjure up, appropriate to your need, spell or ritual, works.

So, you have prepared the altar, cast a circle, made up some simple rhyme, describing what you are doing, 'telling' the herbs, candles, crystals, what it is you wish them to do. What are the other elements of ritual?

Throughout time, religious ceremony has involved the taking of refreshment or the making of offerings in the presence of the deities. In the Craft this has become the 'Cakes and Ale'. Whether your chalice contains ale, wine (home brewed or otherwise), spring water or fruit juice, the partaking of the sacred drink is a major part of the ceremony. The food and drink is ritually blessed and consumed, thereby imparting the blessings of the Goddess and God onto the witch. This practice is echoed in almost every religion in one form or another.

Music is also an important part of ritual, to set the mood and assist in setting free your subconscious energy. There are many tapes and CDs on the market designed for ritual or meditation use, but again, whatever seems right to you.

Finally, whilst you aren't going to dismiss, the elementals and Goddess and God, it is important to psychologically 'end' the rite and what better way than to say a simple 'Thank you'?

The remainder of this chapter is in the form of 'suggested' rituals only. By all means use them until such time as you feel that you want to create your own, or do your own thing from the start. They will set the tone for the particular ritual and hopefully give you ideas for your own rites. They include the casting of circles, standard rites for the Full Moon, the

Sabbats, Rites of Passage i.e. birth, death, a rite of consecration and rite of self-dedication.

Suggested spells and rites for other occasions and needs appear in Hocus Pocus and Eye of Newt.

# 9. Casting a Circle

Prepare the altar appropriately. Individual ideas are given in the rites that follow.

Ground or centre yourself. A simple way to do this is to kick off your shoes and feel the ground beneath your bare feet. Take a few deep breaths and draw in energy from around you as you breathe in, 'see' it flowing down through you, out of the soles of your feet and into the ground.

Now direct your energy outwards to invite the elementals and deities and to draw your 'circle' (remember it's a sphere).This can be done simply by pointing your index finger (usually the power finger) and 'seeing' the light/energy coming from it, or you can do the same with your wand, or your magick knife.
The elementals are invited at their own points of the compass. Where you start is again fraught with tradition and alternatives. Some begin in the North believing that it is from the North that the power flows. Some begin in the east, as I do, acknowledging the East as the direction for the rising of the sun and therefore associating it with the rise of energy or power. That one you must decide for yourself. For the purpose of this text I will begin in the East.

Face East and invite the Air elementals to be present.

> *'Spirits of the East and the elementals of Air, I invite you to take your place and be present at this rite. Welcome.'*

Face the South

*'Spirits of the South and the elementals of Fire, I invite you to take your place and be present at this rite. Welcome.'*

Face the West

*'Spirits of the West and elementals of Water, I invite you to take your place and be present at this rite. Welcome.'*

Face North

*'Spirits of the North and elementals of Earth, I invite you to take your place and be present at this rite. Welcome.'*

At each invitation, try to visualise the elementals; the Earth gnomes, the Air sylphs, the Fire salamanders and the Water undines (mermaid-like creatures).

Now 'draw' your circle or sphere. Walk clockwise around the perimeter of your circle three times, drawing the energy and chanting the following rhyme or something similar.

*'With powers of body and magickal blade,*
*Three times around and the circle is made.*
*Contain all the power, protect from all shade,*
*I conjure you now, pour forth from my blade.'*

Next, invite the Goddess and God to join you.

*'I invite you here, who'll teach me well,*
*All charms and healing, magick and spell.*
*Goddess Fourfold and the Horned One your Lord*
*Come now together in deed and in word.*
*Mistress of Midnight and Master of Dark*

*Kindle my heart with divinities spark.'*

To the Goddess

*'You are the Maiden, youthful and bright*
*Enchantment is yours, first crescent of night.*
*You are the Mother, abundant and ripe,*
*Fertility yours, the giver of life.*
*You are the Crone, last crescent pale*
*Wisdom is yours though waning and frail.*
*You are the Dark Lady, gone is your light,*
*Renewing and resting on this darkest night.*
*You are the Goddess, four faces have you*
*Maid, Mother, Crone and Dark Lady too.*

To the Horned God

*You are the Horned God of deep forest glade*
*Some call you the Dark One, the Lord of the Shades.*
*At Imbolc you sow your seed in the Mother,*
*At Beltane you wed her forsaking all other.*
*At Lammas you bow your head to her scythe*
*As your blood feeds the earth that men will survive.*
*At Samhain you feast without fear or dread*
*As the veil draws aside on this night of the Dead.*
*I remember all life in a circle is bound*
*The eternal return, like seeds in the ground.*
*So, at Yule you are born as the Sun God above*
*Reborn and youthful in search of your love.*
*And at Imbolc you sow your seed in the Mother*
*As above, so below, the goddesses lover.*

Bless the food and wine if they are to be part of your rite. Take your magickal knife and place it, point downwards, into the wine.

*'With feminine cup and masculine blade*
*Unite now the two and a blessing is made.'*

Lightly touch the food, whether it is bread, cakes, cookies, whatever is appropriate to the rite.

*'Bless this food that I may taste your bounty.'*

Perform your rite or ritual or cast your spell. Thank the Goddess and God and the elementals for their presence. Blow out the candles and leave the altar.

If you are casting your super-circle follow the above procedure but 'see' your energies reaching the boundaries of your home, whether it is a wall, a fence, a river, pathway etcetera. To give your super-circle extra strength you can walk the boundaries, sprinkling some salt (earth), water (water), carry an incense stick (air and fire) as you go. This reinforces the edge of the circle with the four elements.

# Yule Rites

Prepare your altar. Candles on this occasion can be red, white or dark green. Decorate with evergreens, holly, and ivy, Christmas tree lights, candles. Yule is the celebration of the birth of the Sun God and the return of light and life to the earth, the turning of the winter towards the spring, so the more light the better. Yule incense should be of cinnamon, spices, orange oil. Flowers can be Poinsettias or Christmas Roses. If you use an altar cloth, reds and greens and golds are appropriate. Appropriate music includes medieval or Gregorian chanting, I personally love the Medieval Babes at Yule. Food on the altar should be seasonal, dried fruits, fruit cake, or spiced cookies, maybe some mulled wine.

If you have been able to keep the Christmas tree dressing etc until now, tonight is the night to bring it indoors and place the baubles and lights on it, encouraging the sun's return. If not, now is the time to place the star, fairy (the symbol of the Goddess) on the top.

Cast your circle up to the blessing of the wine and food. Now we acknowledge the goddesses absence from us, and her return to give birth to the sun.

*'Though worlds have slept, the Goddess kept*
*Her vigil over the Earth.*
*Though icy winds blew, Her children knew*
*She awaited the sun's rebirth.*
*She laboured in dark, to bring forth the spark*
*To give warmth and life to the Earth.*

*Now dark and cold perish, the Sun God we cherish,*
*With joy we acknowledge His birth.*
*Darkness is banished, the light is reborn*
*The Sun grows stronger with every new dawn.*
*Our Goddess has given Her gift to Her clan*
*The Sun God returns to bring warmth to the land.*
*So the Wheel turns once more at this Season of Joy*
*Now winter is ending, No dark can destroy*
*The hope for tomorrow, For peace on our Earth*
*Dark and cold vanish with the Sun God's rebirth.*

*The wheel turns, the power burns.*

Thank the Goddess and God and the elementals for their presence, blow out the candles and leave the altar.

Place candles or fairy lights in the windows to bring back light.

# Imbolc Rites

Prepare the altar. Candles can be white or spring green. Altar cloths are usually white. Snowdrops are the flower of choice and other decorations can include seeds scattered around on the altar. Incense should be sensuous or earthy such as Patchouli. Imbolc is the celebration of the mating of the Goddess and God. Food on the altar should be 'white', lightly baked cookies, or white iced cakes.

Cast your circle up to the blessing of the wine and food.

*'I cast this circle of magick tonight*
*To honour the union of the Goddess bright*
*With the Horned God of forests and dark woodland glade*
*With lance and with grail their magick is made.*
*Silver Lady of moonlit skies*
*Your name upon the wild wind sighs*
*Draw near and feel His passion searing*
*Lay with him now in woodland clearing*
*A union of God and Goddess young*
*A courtship and love from Earth be sprung.*
*You are the maiden, virgin and true*
*Before ploughing your furrow, first He must woo*
*He'll become the great Pan with mischief and fun*
*Play His pipes for you now and the wild chase is won.*
*Will you join with him now and receive of His seed*
*As above so below, you both have decreed*
*The Horned God will lay in your loving embrace*

*As you plough a new furrow beyond time and space*
*He'll sow now the seed of tomorrow's rebirth*
*As life also stirs in the belly of earth.*

Seeds, representing your desires, wishes, ideas or goals that were only theories at Yule, are planted now. Sow the seeds in a pot of compost and leave close to the altar or on a sunny windowsill. Watch them grow, and as they do, so too, do your goals for the coming year.

Thank the Goddess and God, blow out the candles and leave the altar. Light all the lights in the house and leave them all alight for a few moments before turning them off again.

# Ostara Rites

Prepare your altar. Ostara is the celebration of returning fertility to the earth. Decorate the altar with painted eggs, chocolate eggs, fluffy easter chicks or bunnies. Babies bootees could be included if you have them. Daffodils are the flower of choice along with spring greenery, appearing now in parks and gardens everywhere. Spring is well and truly here. Incense should be of spring flowers, light and airy fragrances. Candles are usually yellow as are altar cloths. Altar food should be seasonal.

Ostara is a time for spring cleaning, physical and mental. It is a time of new growth before which we must clear out all the old and unwanted in our lives. Young lambs wobble about the fields on unsteady legs and the first buds are on the trees. The seasons are turning again and Ostara marks the midpoint of spring, from here on in we can start looking forward to summer.

Cast your circle up to the blessing of the food and wine. Light a yellow candle in the cauldron and sit and meditate on what is unwanted and outworn in your life. Write on a piece of paper any habits, thoughts, or unfinished projects, 'see' them disappearing from your life as you burn the paper in the cauldron.

> 'Clean house and clean home,
> Clean away all that's outgrown.
> Spring is turning, summer's coming
> Beasts bear young and flower's growing.
> The Goddess shows her face once more

*In greening fields and sandy shore*
*Darkness lost the age-old fight*
*Succumbing to the summer's light.*
*Thank you for the Winter vanished*
*Days are longer, dark is banished.*
*To summer soon upon the land*
*Life holds out a welcome hand.*

*The wheel turns, the power burns.*

Take your broom and ritually sweep away any remaining mental and psychic clutter. Thank the Goddess and God and the elementals for their presence. Blow out the candles whilst visualising physical and mental cobwebs disappearing. Leave the altar.

# Beltane Rite

Prepare your altar. Beltane sees the marriage of the Goddess and God and is also the beginning of summer, so an abundance of flowers and pretty candles is called for on this occasion. A small piece of white gauze or lace representing the bridal veil of the Goddess can be a part of the decor. Incense should be light and fragrant. It is the one time when it is all right to bring Hawthorn into the home, so place it on the altar and enjoy the fragrance of the May blossom.

Beltane is about fertility as the symbolism of the Maypole shows. The Goddess and God are now married and their fertility is seen all around us. Summer begins, flowers and crops are growing. Creative projects should be reaching fruition now, the seeds planted at Imbolc are thriving. It is a good time for creative magick and fertility magick whether it is for the conception of a child or any other venture.

*'The circle is cast and the time has come*
*For the God and Goddess to join as now one.*
*The Horned God of forests and dark woodland glade*
*Pursued the young Goddess through sunlight and shade.*
*Now time is eternal and love is unwound*
*For the God and his Goddess as their union is bound.*
*Hearts are now kindled and passions afire*
*Mystery of Mysteries are love and desire.*

*She tamed the wild God with the gentlest of heart*
*Blissful in marriage, never to part.*

*By seed root and stem did they promise each other*
*Eternal return and forsake every other.*
*With stars as their witness and earth as their bed*
*The God and the Goddess in truth now are wed.*

Thank the Goddess and God and the elementals for their presence. Blow out the candles and leave the altar.

# Litha Rite (midsummer)

Midsummer shows the Goddess in all her glory. The Sun is at its height and this is the longest day. After this day the darkness begins to regain its hold over the land and the autumn is not too far away. It is the time of culmination in all of our projects and goals. It is a time of purification as the sun's fire is at its most potent. The altar candles and cloth should be red, orange or gold, reflecting the height of the sun's power. Chamomile and lavender make good incense for midsummer.

The summer solstice is a good time to take a firm grip on any really difficult problems that have seemed without solution. This is a festival of the sun and as the sun is primal male energy it is also a good time and for casting spells for male members of the family or friends. This is definitely one occasion for celebrating outside in a garden, woodland, park or on the beach with a picnic.

Cast your circle up to the blessing of the wine and cakes.

*'Summer now is at it's height*
*The sun burns with power and might*
*Its flames are felt on earth below*
*As trees bear fruit and crops all grow.*

*Summer soon will leave the earth*
*And winter waits to kindle hearths*
*The wheel is turning on this day*
*The sun will soon be on its way.*

*To be reborn again in Spring*
*An end to cold and winter bring.*
*But at this hour of power and light*
*I thank the Sun God for His might.*


Thank the Goddess and God and the elementals for their presence. Blow out the candles and leave the altar.

# Lammas Rite

Lammas is my favourite time of year. It is the time of the first harvest and the time when the God sacrifices himself to ensure the harvest and the continuing survival of his people. A time of plenty and the beginning of Autumn. The harvest is gathered and the people begin to look to the winter, to prepare for the cold dark days and to preserve the crops to feed them during the coming winter. Now, we just go to Tesco's as normal and the shift of the seasons is remarkable only by the soap operas and the time at which we turn on our lights.

But to the witch, Lammas is a time for thanksgiving, for the crops, for the Goddess who is temporarily still with us and for the sacrifice of the God to nourish his people.

Prepare the altar with candles of gold, and altar cloths are also of gold or orange. Loaves of bread, bought or home baked adorn the altar and if you are lucky enough to get hold of some ears of wheat or maize, then they should have pride of place on your altar.

*'Lammas night, Harvest Home*
*Winds have blown, the sun has shone*
*The corn is high, the Harvest nigh*
*The trees bear fruit in abundance hung*
*Blessings above on earth are sprung.*

*Summer's harvest, winter's store*
*Food and bounty, want no more*
*From the mother's womb the harvest come*

*For winter's need, her kin to feed.*
*Our spirits too from Earth are fed*
*Near to light and free from dread*
*All thanks to Thee our Mother Earth*
*For your Harvest soon to birth.*

*The God has bent his head to your scythe*
*His blood feeds the earth for his clan to survive*
*We thank him now for his precious gift*
*As the golden corn and crops we lift.*

*Our daily bread and staff of life*
*Sustains us all through good and strife*
*The God of the corn is departed from sight*
*To be reborn at Yule as the Sun God of light.'*

Make offerings to the Goddess and the sacrificed God of bread and milk and honey. Place them in a small bowl and leave it outside for passing animals such as cats or hedgehogs.

*'Receive this offering before I depart*
*Strengthened in body, mind and heart.'*

Thank the Goddess and God and the elementals as normal. Blow out the candles and leave the altar.

# Mabon Rite (autumn equinox)

The days and nights are equal again and the autumn is half over. Days are getting shorter and the sun's strength is diminished as chilly winds blow in from the North. The leaves are falling from the trees and we can taste winter in the air. It is the second harvest when the last of the fruits and the grains are gathered and the earth begins its annual rest.

It is the time for reaping the rewards of our labours throughout the year. Anything that is unresolved is dealt with now, grievances and quarrels should be laid to rest. It is a time of letting go, and if necessary lamenting what went unfulfilled. Grieve for it and let it go, ready to begin again refreshed at Imbolc.

The altar is prepared and dressed with fallen leaves and branches, fruits and vegetables that are harvested now for winter. Candles and altar cloths are usually in autumnal colours of reds, orange and brown. Incense can be of sage, chrysanthemum, pine, lemon.

Cast the circle to the blessing of the wine.

*'The harvest is gathered and the barns are full*
*The earth will rest now until spring comes again*
*We thank Mother earth for her bounty once more*
*Food for the winter, for bread and for grain.*

*Leaves fall softly now that summer is dead*
*Covering the ground in a carpet of rust*
*But after every cold winter the spring will awake*
*The eternal return, in the Goddess we trust.*

*The birds fly south to climes warm and mild*
*Fields are ploughed under to lie ridged and fallow.*
*We prepare for the winter and kindle our hearth*
*To dream of the spring and the return of the swallow.*

*Summer's death is greeted with joy,*
*Rejoicing and feasting, no sign of sorrow.*
*The wheel of the year must continue to turn*
*From dark will come light and hope for tomorrow.*

*Out of death comes life, out of darkness light, out of winter*
*comes spring.*
*The wheel turns, the power burns.*

Thank the Goddess and God and the elementals as usual.
Blow out the candles and leave the altar.

# Samhain Rite

Samhain, All Hallows Eve, Halloween. Perhaps the most well known pagan festival and the one most associated with witches. Unfortunately it has gathered to itself a sinister reputation as children parade dressed as ghosts and ghouls and in recent times, serial killers and monsters from the big screen as once again we have lost sight of the true meaning of Halloween.

Samhain is the time when the veil between the worlds is thin and fragile and spirits are able to contact this plane of existence. It is the time when we remember our loved ones who have departed this life and await rebirth in the Summerlands. Perhaps it is these associations that make it a good time to come to terms with ageing and our own mortality.

In times past beasts were slaughtered at Samhain for food for the winter and great feasts took place to show that the people had no fear of the winter, in their knowledge that the wheel would turn and the spring would come again, bringing new life to the land.

Prepare the altar with candles of orange or gold, and altar cloths of the same hue. Pumpkins carved into Jack-O-Lanterns and left in their natural state surrounded by dried, fallen leaves adorn the altar along with photographs of any departed loved ones. Apples too are traditional at this time. There is a definite shift in energies at this time as the year is dying and the sacrificed God is in the Underworld. He waits for the Goddess as Persephone to go down into the Underworld to him and soon the face of the Goddess too is lost from the land. Chrysanthemums are the flowers of the dead so are appropriate at this time to appear as altar decoration or used in incense.

*'The veil is thin and frail this night*
*As spirits roam in search of light*
*Jack O Lantern grins and glares*
*into the dark as his candle flares*
*To keep us safe from harm or plight*
*And bane and evil put to flight.*
*Welcome now the ancestors home*
*To share the fireside they come.*

*The year is dead, the year is over*
*No sign of the God and his Lady lover*
*But tomorrow comes and a new year's dawn*
*Brings hope for the day when they will return.*
*The cycle of life is once more revolving*
*In ending, beginning, always evolving.*

*The wheel turns, the power burns.*

Thank the deities and the elementals as normal but leave the altar candles alight to burn themselves out. Place them in the bath or the kitchen sink for safety.

So the eight sabbats of the year have been and gone and once again it will soon be time for Yule, when the Sun God is reborn and light and life return to the Mother Earth. By celebrating these turning points of the year and being aware of our place in the scheme of things we move that much closer to the Goddess herself.

# A Rite for the Full Moon

Silver light floods the woodland glade as cooling rays of moonlight illuminate the ground. The moon is round and the tides are high. It is the first night of the full moon. For many centuries witches have gathered or worked alone on this night, recognising the maturity of the Goddess as she rides the midnight sky. She is in her phase of the Mother at this time, and abundance and fertility are the keynotes of their magick.

Some have recently come to the conclusion that she is static at this time, having already travelled through her phases to become full and round. For three nights she is going nowhere until she begins her waning phase until she is finally lost from sight at the dark of the moon and so some modern witches prefer simply to acknowledge her beauty at this time rather than cast spells but magick can never be motionless in my opinion

Whilst She appears to be static, I believe that there can never be a complete lack of movement in nature, however subtle, and that includes the cycles of the moon. Traditionally, the full moon is a time for creating magick connected with fertility and abundance, for things coming to fruition and I, for one, carry on the tradition.

This is another of those signposts folks, and an issue that you must decide for yourself. Like I said in the beginning there are no hard and fast rules in the Craft, except for harming none, and that is why witches and the Craft will always evolve and change in a subtle way around the old traditions.

The moon is full for three successive nights, plenty of opportunity to snatch a few minutes for the following rite.

This can of course be combined with the casting of spells should you so wish.

Prepare the altar with white or silver candles and altar cloths of the same colour. If you cannot get outside for this rite, or you cannot see Her because of cloud or any other reason, place a silver coin on the altar to represent Her in Her silver fullness.

Cast the circle up to the blessing of the wine.

*'Silver Lady, riding high,*
*Sacred Jewel of Midnight sky*
*Cooling rays shine from above*
*Illuminating all with love.*

*Sleeping village and City street*
*Woodland dell where rivers meet*
*All are bathed in silver light*
*Magick spells are cast this night.*
*The Mother shows her face to all*
*For fertility now on Her we call*

*Abundance now from Her is granted*
*Magick freed and spell enchanted.*
*Soon Her light and power wane*
*The Crone can then be seen again*
*Then darkness rules the midnight sky*
*'Til sickle moon appears on high.*

*Then She grows in light and power*
*'Til once again the magick hour*
*When silver light floods hill and plain*
*The Mother has returned again.*

Thank the Goddess in particular this night, tell her how beautiful She is. Blow out the candles and leave the altar.

# A Rite of Self-Dedication

There comes a time when you know that you have to give yourself to the Craft and to the Goddess and God. It happens at different times for everyone, but you will not mistake the time when it comes. Perform this rite whenever you feel the need but I would avoid carrying it out at the same time as a Sabbat or other rite.

It manifests as a desire to do or say something meaningful and can be as simple as lighting a candle and just sitting quietly by your altar, allowing Her to come close to you to absorb what you are feeling. It can be a loving act of tending a wild area or a walk in the park with your children, 'seeing' Her with different eyes for the first time. One thing you should prepare for though, is the overwhelming emotion that this rite will bring. I recommend a box of Kleenex be close by! Prepare the altar with white candles and flowers or leaves that are in season and burn your favourite incense. Some witches take a Craft or 'hidden' name at this point. If you feel comfortable with that then by all means do so, but it is not essential. Remember the Goddess knows us, whatever name we choose to go by. An additional candle should be placed centrally.

Cast your circle up to the blessing of the wine.

*I ..................... come before you my Lady and Lord to dedicate myself to you. I promise to do whatever I can to live up to your ways and ask that you be patient as I walk your path. If I wander away or fall aside, pick me back up, dust me down and send me on my way again. Guide me and teach me the ways of the Old Ones, the innocence and fun of the Maiden, the love and patience of the Mother, the wisdom of the Crone. May*

*I watch your faces and phases on the Earth and in the Moon and the Sun. May I see you reflected in my own phases and cycles and give me understanding of each of them.*

If you have a particular interest in one aspect of the Craft, such as Herbal Magick or Potion brewing, you could ask for help and guidance as you learn those ways.

Drink a toast to the Goddess and God and to your future as a witch.

Light the central candle and surround yourself with its light. Sit quietly for a time absorbing the calm atmosphere until you feel that the rite is over. Thank the Goddess and God and the elementals, blow out the altar candles but leave the central candle alight. As before, place it in the bath or the kitchen sink to burn itself out safely, the fire brigade has no place in this ritual!

# The Rite of Wiccanning (or Presenting)

I want to say right from the beginning, that a child of a witch is not 'promised' to the Goddess and God and is not indoctrinated into the Old Religion. A child is not our property and their future spirituality is not for us to decide. This simple rite is simply an introduction of the child to the Goddess and God, a request for blessings on them, for protection as they grow until such time as they can see for themselves their own spiritual path.

I have two sons, both grown with children of their own, and I have never at any time insisted that they read or learn about the Craft or the Old Religion. Yes, they grew up in a home that was full of love for the Goddess but they never attended any rite or ritual until I believed that they were mature enough to do so.

Living the ways of the cottage witch was a natural way of life for me, and seeing the home alight with candles and bedecked in flowers and leaves, (not to mention strange smells in the kitchen!) the home always reflecting the seasons and natural cycles was nothing out of the ordinary for them. They were given the opportunity to investigate orthodox religions and attend Church if they so wished and their questions were answered simply and honestly and without prejudice. They have matured to adulthood with a respect for nature and a recognition of the part that nature plays in our lives and I like to think that they will pass that same respect and caring to their own children.

I say these things to you because it is only natural that you will be concerned about the implications of your 'Craft' on your family. There is no need to be concerned providing that you always remember that what is the right path for one, is not necessarily right for another, no matter how much you love them.

Having said all of those things it is only natural that you will want to show your child to the Goddess just as you would to a favourite Aunt or doting Granny. She is after all the Mother of us all.

Prepare your altar with white candles and flowers. Place a candle centrally for lighting later in the rite.

*'Gentle Goddess and Powerful God, I bring to you this child ............. (name). I ask for your protection and strength as he/she grows in light and love. Watch over him/her as she moves from an infant to child and child to adult until such time as he/she can choose his/her own path, whatever that may be.*

*Gentle Goddess I ask you to bestow the gift of beauty and gentleness to this child.*
*Powerful God, I ask you to give strength and courage to this child to see him/her through any adversity.*
*Elementals of Earth give him/her a solid foundation on which to grow.*
*Elementals of Air give power to his/her thoughts.*
*Elementals of Fire give warmth and the power of transformation to him/her.*
*Elementals of Water give this child stability in his/her emotions.*
*Light the central candle.*

*By the powers of Earth, Air, Fire and Water and with the love and strength of the Goddess and God I light this flame as a symbol of the light that this child brings to the world. May he/she be forever blessed. '*

After a few moments blow out the candle. This can be kept safely and lit on every birthday, or at any time that you feel that the child needs a bit of extra 'watching over'.

Thank Them as usual and blow out the altar candles.

Children are indeed a gift of the Goddess but they are only borrowed for a short space of time. In that time we can only give them light and love and the space to grow as an individual.

# Rite of Handfasting

In days past, the rite of handfasting was valid for a year and a day. It probably saved many a divorce! In recent times however, the option to handfast for a year and a day is still there although many wiccan couples actually pledge themselves together for this life and the life to come, to travel together as soul mates. Any religious ceremony of promise does have far reaching effects and this rite especially needs to be taken very seriously. If a couple pledge themselves together for all time and lives and subsequently part then perhaps on the surface the situation may have been accepted, psychologically there may be far reaching problems. My husband and I are handfasted for all times and lives and we know that we have shared many lives in the past but if this is not the case, then I would urge any couple to be very sure before making this commitment.

I have written this rite in the format for a couple to make their own commitment of handfasting without the presence of others. You will need a length of cord or ribbon for this rite, as the hands are bound together (hand fasted) and your broom. If it is planned to exchange rings, they should be placed on the altar, on the pentacle (plate).

Cast the circle up to the blessing of the wine.

Female witch: *May this place be sacred to the Goddess and the God as we stand here to be joined in the rite of handfasting.*

Male witch: *So must it be.*

Female Witch: *May the beings of Air be with us and tie the bonds between closely.*

Male Witch: *May the beings of fire bring passion to our union.*

Female Witch: *May the beings of water bring the depth of the oceans and purity of the mountain spring to our love.*

Male Witch: *May the beings of Earth bring stability to our love.*

Both: *May the Goddess and God bless our union.*

Female Witch: *All Goddesses are one Goddess and the wise call her 'Woman' or 'Mother, She is the creator and she brings desire to the Father, the Horned God.*

Male Witch: *Let me look in the face of this woman and see in Her the Goddess in all her phases, all her beauty and all her love.*

Female Witch: *............ will you take me, to your hand and your heart as your bride and comforter in this life and those to come?*

Male Witch: *I will. .................... will you take me, to your hand and your heart as your husband and protector in this life and those to come?*

If rings are to be exchanged, take them from the altar and place them on each other's fingers at this point. Take the cord or ribbon, place the palms of your left hands together and with your free right hands, bind the hands together loosely.

Female Witch: *I give you my hand, my heart and my spirit at the setting of the sun, the rising of the stars and in the name of the Goddess now and for all lives and times. Death will not part us, for we shall be born again and meet and know and love again.*

Male Witch: *I give you my hand, my heart and my spirit at the setting of the sun and the rising of the stars and in the name of the Horned God now and for all lives and times. Death will not part us, for we shall be born again and meet and know and love again.*

Kiss each other and unwind the cord or ribbon. Cut it into two halves with your white handled knife and each takes half for safe keeping.

Place the broomstick parallel to the altar, hold each others hand and jump over the broom. (The origin of the saying living over the brush. )

If the handfasting is to be for a year and a day, simply substitute the words 'for all lives and times' with something more appropriate.

Congratulations!

# Requiem Rite

Every rite of passage should be marked with ritual. It is the way that the human psyche makes sense of these occasions. Sometimes the occasions are painful as we lose a loved one and it is hard not to grieve for them as they invariably leave a large hole in our lives. It is not in an attempt to fill that hole that we turn to ritual but a way to accept their loss and to hand them over to another plane of existence.

Remember that all life is a cycle and the eternal return, like the seeds in the ground, ensuring that we will be born and live again. Life will always follow death and will also one day end again.

The requiem rite is not a rite of sorrow but of release and thanks for the time that they shared with us this time around.

Prepare your altar with candles of your loved ones favourite colour, and decorate with their favourite flowers. Place on the altar a jug or other ceramic vessel, a small hammer, a container big enough to hold the jug and a central candle, which should be lit in readiness.

Cast the circle up to the blessing of the wine.

*'Our bodies are but a vessel in which we journey towards the light. As life is extinguished and ................... is no longer in our sight, he / she will remain in our hearts.*

*We give thanks for the joy that they brought to us, the lessons that they taught us and the comfort that they gave us. Now is the time for their release for them to move on and grow in the company of the Goddess until they will be born again.*

*The vessel of the body is no longer necessary as their spirit lives on in us and around us.* '

Place the jug into the container, take the hammer and break the jug with it.

Extinguish the central candle.

' *His / her light is extinguished from this world but is a beacon in the Summerland. May it shine again.*'

Spend some time remembering pleasant times and happy occasions shared with him or her.

Thank the Goddess and God and the elementals for their presence and support at this difficult time. Blow out the altar candles and leave the altar.

Take the broken vessel and bury it in the garden or in a large terracotta pot. Plant seeds or transplant a flower and as it grows remember the eternal return.

# 9. Parsley, Sage, Rosemary and Thyme

*Parsley, Sage, Rosemary and Thyme*
*These are all such good friends of mine*
*Sage for wisdom, Thyme for health*
*Apple for love and Basil for wealth.*
*These friends aplenty in my garden grow*
*To bring me luck or make the winds blow.*
*Such treasures in life are there to be found*
*Flowering brightly or under the ground.*
*Garlic and lemon, onion and pea*
*Nature's harvest given to me.*
*What can we want for? What can we need?*
*If only the lessons of herbs we would heed.*

Herbs have been the tools and best friends of the witch since the dawn of time. The power that they contain will heal, enchant, banish negativity and bring cheer and prosperity. Herbal charms have been found in archeological digs dating back to the Stone Age. It is only in recent years that the human race has discarded and lost respect for these wonderful life forms in the name of science, using them only as flavourings in otherwise bland cooking that contains no magick. Herbal medicine and herbal magick have gone hand in hand since the first woman or man picked the green leaf and found its energies were there to be harnessed for the good of everyone.

Anyone can make friends of the herbs, grow them in your garden, or a pot on the windowsill, use them fresh, or dry them, buy them from your local supermarket, however you obtain them, use them.

Ancient magickal spells and parchments have called for all sorts of weird and wonderful herbs and even today in the most modern of magick books there appears an array of hard to get herbs, sold by out of the way occult stores, available to most only by mail order. Remember our friend the cottage witch? She had no such stores and the postman certainly didn't knock on her door with brown paper parcels containing her magickal ingredients. Nope, she went into her garden and pulled a few parsley leaves, or basil for her spell to bring her a bit of prosperity. She crushed garlic and strung the flowers of the garlic plant to rid herself of negativity or bad luck. She would place a halved onion in her home if she wanted something banished, as onion absorbs all forms of negativity, including some harmful bacteria! The reason why once an onion is cut it should be used or thrown away.

So, on the next trip to the supermarket, cast your eyes along the herb shelves and instead of seeing, dried green leaves to just sprinkle on your soup, see the power to treat cystitis, a banishing herb, a way to attract some wealth into your life. Magick indeed.

A word of caution however, only minor ailments should be treated with home herbal remedies. Anything more serious than colds or 'flu, sore throats and minor infections should be treated by a qualified medical or herbal practitioner. Also any symptoms that persist or change in any way should be considered beyond home remedies.

Herbs can be used medicinally in teas, tinctures, oils and infusions. All of these methods are discussed in the chapter Hocus Pocus and Eye of Newt as are their magickal uses.

Remember too, the early lesson of asking permission before picking or cutting anything that is growing. Respect for the herbs is important, it is very likely giving up its life for our benefit, so a word of thanks is the least we can give in return.

## Parsley
Folk name: Devil's Oatmeal.

There are two main types of parsley, curly leaf and flat leaf. Both have the same properties medicinally and magickally although the flat leaf variety has more flavour.

Parsley seeds are very slow to germinate, sometimes taking up to six weeks to appear as shoots above the earth and it is this that gave it the legend of going down to the devil seven times before germination, hence its name of Devil's Oatmeal. Other lore tells us that Parsley grows best where the woman rules the household, and also that you should never plant parsley seeds in your own garden, but steal the plant from someone else's. Probably due to the length of time it takes to germinate, pinching a ready grown plant removes the problem. Remember the Law of Return though, nicking a plant from another garden is not to be recommended!

Medicinally, Parsley is a very effective diuretic, making it an excellent treatment for minor bouts of cystitis and kidney infections This quality also makes it an effective friend in any weight loss programme. It is a digestive tonic, getting rid of painful wind or colic and is also an excellent breath freshener. It will help to bring on menstruation and for this reason, large quantities of parsley should not be consumed if pregnant as it could cause a miscarriage.

Parsley is also a good first aid treatment for wounds or insect bites. A handful of parsley leaves crushed and placed onto a bite, will reduce any swelling, neutralise any poison and get

**103**

rid of the pain. Laying Parsley onto a wound and covering it with a clean cloth helps to stop the bleeding in a wound and also reduces the risk of any infection.

Plant parsley close to tomatoes and roses but never near carrots as it attracts carrot fly.

Magickally, Parsley is an herb of protection, purification and induces lust. It is reputed to stop misfortune from appearing in your life. The Romans used to put parsley onto plates with food to stop any contamination, this is carried through today as a garnish but the origin of the practice was for safety!

It was said that parsley would heal sick fish if thrown into the water, probably due to its high mineral content. Still, next time Goldie looks a bit off colour, give it a whirl.

Planting parsley was believed to be a sure way to conceive a child, and bathing in water with parsley is one way to connect with the Mother aspect of the Goddess.

It is also an herb associated with the Underworld and therefore used in funerary rites such as the Requiem Rite and by association is an herb used at Samhain.

Parsley tea is made by steeping 2 tsp of dried herb in half a pint of boiling water for 15 minutes, then straining and drinking. **This should not be taken internally if pregnant.**


**Sage**
Folk name: Wise One

Sage is long associated with wisdom and we carry on that association in current vocabulary. A sage is a wise person and the word sagacity, implies wisdom.

**104**

There are several types of Sage, Common or Garden Sage is the most widely available, especially in its dried form from the supermarket shelf. Then we have Red Sage, Purple Sage and White Sage. The white sage is the variety most used by the Native American Indians especially the dried stalks which are bound together and smouldered (smudging) for purification purposes.

Sage is associated with long life and well being. There is an old English proverb which states 'Eat Sage in May, live forever and a day' and a Roman proverb 'Why should a man die if he has Sage in his garden?' Its Latin name is Salvia which means 'saviour'.

Really, Sage is deserving of a chapter all to itself, but the essence of this book is simplicity and the herbs are explored in greater detail in future books.

Sage is a natural disinfectant, antibacterial and stops bleeding when crushed and placed on a wound. Sage has long been a substitute for tea and was so highly prized in times past that one chest of sage would be exchanged for three of China tea.

It sharpens the intellect, promotes brain activity, clears and purifies the blood and smoked it is an effective treatment for asthma (current medical thinking may take issue with that but I think I would prefer to give it a go rather than inhale steroids). Sage will reduce fevers when taken as an infusion or tea and is said to have anti-ageing properties. I think this is due to its positive effect on the brain, he who thinks young stays young.

A sage leaf rubbed on the teeth will whiten them and an infusion of sage is an effective mouthwash or gargle in the treatment of mouth ulcers, sore throats and tonsillitis. It is also effective in the treatment of rheumatism and arthritis when made into a liniment and rubbed onto aching joints and muscles. This can be achieved by making up a rubbing oil from an eggcup of olive oil to which has been added several drops of Sage oil.

Sage tea can be prepared by infusing 2 teaspoons of the dried herb in a half pint of water for fifteen minutes. Sage is another herb that should not be taken internally in this manner whilst pregnant.

Magickally, Sage is protective and purifying. Write a wish on a Sage leaf and put it under your pillow. Sleep on it for three nights and if you dream of your wish it will come true. If Sage thrives in your garden so will your business. If Sage withers and dies there, I'm afraid it's bad news for your accountant! Toads love Sage in the garden so if you're looking for a familiar .......

Grey hair that used to be dark? Rinse your hair repeatedly with a cold infusion of sage and your hair will darken like magick.

Sage is also said to help in loss or grieving, so is an ideal herb to use at Samhain or to help get over the loss of a loved one. Sage is very easy to grow in a pot indoors, so given all the above, I think it's worth a shot, don't you?


**Rosemary**
Folk Name: Mary's Mantle.

Rosemary is an herb of protection and purification associated as it is with the Virgin Mary. It is cleansing and drives away negative influences, but primarily it is known as an herb of remembrance. For this reason it is used in all rituals and ceremonies that you wish to remember. It is used in bridal bouquets and has long been an herb putting in an appearance at funerals and death rites, worn by mourners to remember the one that has passed over.

The heavily fragranced rosemary improves the memory on a physical level and is an excellent remedy for headaches especially those brought on by stress.

Rosemary is very easy to grow, and is one of the herbs that does well in a pot indoors. The cottage witch knew to 'plant Rosemary at the garden gate' to ensure her cottage was protected from thieves and her garden and home would flourish. It holds true today and beautiful Rosemary bushes can be seen in many a cottage garden, standing proudly at the garden gate. No garden? A pot of Rosemary just inside your front door will do just as well, as does a sprig of Rosemary hung indoors.

It is one of the oldest incenses, having been found in Egyptian tombs and also bound into the wrappings of several mummies.

An infusion of Rosemary, or Rosemary tea is a great cure for those who have trouble falling asleep, you know the times when you just can't still your mind as it goes over and over the events of the day or the day ahead. Taken daily as a tonic it helps relieve the pains of rheumatism and arthritis, it is a natural antiseptic and a speedy and efficient gargle and mouthwash, relieving the pain of mouth ulcers almost immediately. It is a circulatory stimulant and a tonic to the digestive tract. Rosemary used externally on dressings or compresses heals wounds, strains and bruises.

The magickal uses of this wonderfully pungent herb include all rites of passage, especially funeral rites and can be used in the ritual cup as an infusion or simply a sprig of the fresh herb in the wine. A wash made of rosemary is an effective way to cleanse and empower ritual tools. Burnt with juniper in a sickroom, Rosemary will speed the healing and recovery of the patient.

Folklore has it that Rosemary attracts fairies.


**Thyme**
Folk name: Old Mother Thyme

Thyme is healing, purifying, gives courage, attracts love and enhances psychic powers.

It relieves sadness and depression, lifting low spirits almost immediately, especially when this state is brought about by events in the past. Just sniffing a bunch of thyme will imbue one with courage and energy. It will help to keep a sense of proportion in times of stress and to keep a light heart when work gets heavy and goals and ambitions are being pursued. Perhaps we all take ourselves a little too seriously, and Thyme is just the herb to help us to laugh at ourselves sometimes. It is a warming herb and therefore of exceptional use in all cold conditions and having an affinity with the lungs helps conditions such as asthma and bronchitis, or simple coughs and colds.

Thyme is another herb that is easy to grow indoors, on a sunny windowsill, it does like a lot of water but not to have its feet wet, so regular watering but don't overdo it.

In addition to being another natural antiseptic, Thyme is an insect repellent, so an excellent herb to grow near a barbecue area! Thyme worn to a funeral will protect from negative emotions that abound on these occasions. It is another herb associated with the fairy folk, who are said to dance in beds of Thyme, and held in the hand whilst calling the fairies, will ensure an answer. Speaking of dancing, Thyme sprinkled into a hot footbath, is brilliant for tired feet, and I don't know any busy career gal or harassed mum who doesn't suffer from that!

## Basil
Folk name: Witch's Herb

Basil is associated with healing, love, protection, exorcism, and flying but primarily lends itself to the attraction of wealth or business.

The strong sweet aniseed like smell of basil is unmistakable and immediately brings the gift of sunshine and happiness. It is a soother of tempers and if brought into a room where a quarrel is taking place, will diffuse the situation. It is said that no evil can exist where basil is. Grown in a pot on the kitchen windowsill, Basil will keep flies from the kitchen. Given as a gift will bring good luck to a new home and gives the gift

Medicinally, as an infusion or tea, Basil is a super tonic that stimulates the digestion and relieves griping stomach pains. It eases frazzled nerves, relieves nausea and headaches, nervous disorders and upset stomachs, especially those associated with migraine.

Magickally, Basil comes into its own in spells concerning prosperity, wealth and business. Every witch that I know that owns a shop or business, keeps Basil in the till or in the Invoice book. A basil leaf kept in the purse ensures that it will never be empty and carried in the pocket will attract good fortune.

## Garlic
Folk Name: Devil's Posy.

Apart from causing extreme anxiety and palpitations to vampires, garlic is a fantastic herb to be used in protective rituals. Its effect on a certain Romanian Count comes from its absolute ability to repel all evil and negativity in no uncertain terms.

Medicinally, Garlic is almost a cure all, and even our orthodox friends in the medical profession are acknowledging its healing powers. For those among us, (including me!) whose cholesterol levels are less than desirable, Garlic will actually reduce the amount of cholesterol in the blood. Taken daily, in food or as capsules (probably better for the social life!) Garlic alleviates the symptoms of rheumatism and arthritis, will ward of colds and 'flu along with most other infections. It contains very high levels of iodine and for this reason is extremely helpful for those with an underactive thyroid.

Hanging a string of garlic in the kitchen will ensure that the entire household is kept free from negative energies, but make sure that it isn't used medicinally or in cooking if hung for this purpose. Folklore tells us that rubbing a clove of garlic over the site of disease will help to bring about a cure. I can't make comment on that except to say that there is nothing to lose in doing this, except possibly a few friends.

Everyone knows the effect of eating garlic, especially the following day, and this can be alleviated by chewing our good friend parsley.

So, without so much as setting foot in an occult supply store or leafing through expensive catalogues, a trip to the supermarket shelf, for not a lot of money, obtains all the necessary herbs to bring about, health, wealth, happiness, protection, purification and blessings. What more can you need?

Whilst the information I have given in this chapter is enough to begin working with the magick of herbs, it is in itself a massive study and there are many excellent books dedicated purely to the use of herbs magickally and medicinally. A list of some of the better ones can be found at the end of this book.

# 10. Candle, Candle, Burning bright

An introduction to Candle Magick.

*Candle, Candle, burning bright*
*Seal my spell with magick light*
*Pink for love, and blue for calm*
*Red for lust, the candle's charm*
*Candle, candle, burning bright,*
*Send my spell into the night.*

The flicker of candlelight evokes warm and cosy, romantic emotions, but there's more going on inside that flame than atmosphere. Transformation is the energy associated with the element of fire, the solid wax is being transmuted into a liquid and eventually evaporated into a gas to become one with the air element. Any magickal working that is associated with the candle is triggered, empowered and released in the simple act of lighting a magickally prepared candle.

The burning of candles forms a major part of many religious ceremonies in many belief systems. The Roman Catholic Church has its banks of petition candles inside the church, candles appear on the altars of all orthodox churches, Buddhist monks light candles to Buddha, all using the transformative powers of fire and light. And what about blowing out your birthday cake candles and making a wish? Candle magick if ever I saw it.

The more of your own energy that you can infuse into the preparation of the candle the better, right down to making your own candles, but realistically this isn't always possible or practical and so buying your candles and preparing them for magick is the next best thing. So now you need to choose the right candle for the job in hand.

## Colour

Colours are associated with different energies and situations and as always there are variations on a theme. To keep things straightforward the table that follows is a simple guide to choosing the right colour for the right spell.

| *Purpose* | *Colour* |
| --- | --- |
| **Healing** | Green |
| **Love** | Pink |
| **Lust** | Red |
| **Peace/Calm** | Pale Blue |
| **Spirituality** | Dark Blue or purple |
| **Money** | Green/Gold |
| **Success** | Gold |
| **To honour the Goddess** | Silver or White |
| **To honour the God** | Gold or Yellow |

## Preparation

The right colour candle has been chosen and now it needs to be prepared or enchanted. The purpose of the spell is carved onto the candle, using the white handled knife, using simple words, symbols or pictures. Runes can be inscribed onto the candle but if your aren't familiar with them, it is far better to

use symbols or words that bring the spell firmly into mind than strange signs that mean nothing to you. If you wish to study the runes and become familiar with their meanings then great, go ahead and inscribe them on your candle. As always, whatever means the most to you, goes.

After inscribing the candle, it is rubbed with oil, prepared specifically for the purpose, bought or made by yourself. Hold the candle in the middle, from the centre of the candle rub the oil outwards towards the end, visualising your magickal intent or goal whilst doing this. Repeat this process, beginning in the centre of the candle and working towards the opposite end, still visualising your magickal intentions. This procedure is known as 'dressing' the candle. The candle should be enchanted at this point by the repetitive repetition of a suitable rhyme, simple but effective in transmitting the spell into the candle. The rhyme may be as simple or elaborate as you wish, or you may simply 'tell' the candle what it's purpose is.

Next, place the candle in a holder, preferably one that is kept solely for this purpose. I have an old pewter candlestick for this, one purchased very cheaply at a car boot sale, complete with battered base, but there was just something about it ..... Place the candle on your altar, preferably on your pentacle or plate, flanked by the two altar candles. Repeat the magickal rhyme and hold the stem of the candle between the palms of your hands, visualise once again the desired outcome of the spell.

Light the candle and release the magick. Allow the candle to burn right down. If you have to leave it unattended, either remove it from the altar and place it safely into the bathtub or sink to complete its task, or blow it out, remembering to send the energy into the air with the smoke, relight it when you can ensure its safe burning. I personally prefer to place the lit candle into the bathtub if I am called away, or if I want it to burn overnight, allowing the spell to be released in one hit.

## Seven Day Candle Spell

Whilst the above simple candle spell is fine for most purposes, sometimes there are problems of a long standing nature that need a steady release of energy. For these occasions, the seven day candle is the ideal solution. It is possible to purchase candles that are made specifically for this, appearing as a 'tower' of seven spheres of wax. This is fine, but in accordance with our 'cottage witch principles' not necessary. Simply take your white handled knife and divide the candle into seven by carving seven equally spaced notches onto the candle. Burn the candle down to the first notch on day one, the second notch on day two, and so on. Each day, before you light the candle, repeat your spell and hold the candle again between the palms of your hands, infusing it with your personal energy and magickal goal.

## Poppet Candles

Poppett candles or image candles can be found in almost all gift shops nowadays, of course they are not sold as such items, simply as novelty candles. I have seen candles moulded into animal forms, perfect for spellworking for a sick or lost pet, a pair of entwined lovers, excellent for love magick, let your imagination go. Alternatively, you can mould and shape your own magickal candles by melting down a taper or church type candle, allowing it to cool, then shaping it like play dough. Thread the wick through a darning needle and push it down through the candle whilst the wax is still soft. Allow the whole thing to become solid. Then proceed as normal and light the candle to release the spell.

## Votive Candles

Votive candles are small tea light type candles or miniature versions of an ordinary candle. These are used when working for a specific person without specific intent, for example, you find yourself thinking of a friend or relative, you want to send your love or energy to them, simply visualise the person, place the votive candle on the altar, light it and send out your love.

## Making your own candles

If you do find yourself with enough time to make your candles, it is really easy. Moulds can be found in your store cupboard in the form of yoghurt cartons, washing up liquid bottles, any plastic container with the right size and shape. Keep the ends of all of your white or cream candles, and when you have enough, melt them down for recycling. The wicks can be made from kitchen type string, but can be found readily and cheaply in craft shops. Colour your candles with wax crayons, add essential oils or herbs to them to give them extra oomph or specific purpose. For example, you need some extra cash fairly rapidly. Melt down the wax, add some dark green wax crayons, some basil oil, a few torn up leaves of basil, run the wick through the mould and add the melted wax mixture. When set, remove it from the mould, empower and enchant it, carve symbols of money onto the outside, pound signs in the United Kingdom, dollars in the States. See your bills marked 'paid' or your bank balance reading as it should do, light the touchpaper and stand well back!

Your spells are limited only by your imagination, use colour, shape and scent to tailor your candles to your magickal needs, so get lighting those wicks and release the magick.

At the risk of repetition and teaching granny to suck eggs, it goes without saying that lit candles should not be left unattended  unless positioned in a place of safety, and away from curtains or other flammable  objects such as scarves that flap about along with the enthusiasm. And yes, there is another ' fire story', but I need to keep some dignity!

# 11. Witchin' in the Kitchen

*Kitchen witchin' is my thing*
*On open fire or electric ring*
*Incense, brews and romantic food*
*Herbal cures to heal my brood*
*Whatsoever is my need today*
*It's to the kitchen I make my way*
*Friends and family here are drawn*
*To gather round the range so warm*
*The kettle sings and cauldron bubbles*
*People come to leave their troubles*
*All are welcome none are banned*
*Refreshed and nurtured by my hand*
*But from the Goddess comes the source*
*With love She reigns in my kitchen, of course.*

The kitchen is the heart of the home. How many times have we heard that? This stems from the days that the principle fire or hearth of the home was in the kitchen, which became a gathering place for the entire family, children were reared in the kitchens due to its warmth, grandmothers passed on their wisdom in the kitchen, either at the table, in front of the oven, or sitting in a comfortable armchair by the range.

The way to a man's heart is through his stomach. Old fashioned maybe, but nevertheless filled with more than a grain of truth. Love potions and food imbued with magickal love energy have often contributed to the ringing of wedding bells.

The woman's domain? Possibly. The witch's domain? Absolutely.

Kitchen lore and magick is abundant and it is the place in the home where most witches' magick begins. From the simple act of making a cup of tea to family breakfast, weight watchers lunch, or a cough remedy for the kids, all have the potential beginnings of magick.

Food in general has its own magick, it sustains life and without it our physical bodies would soon die. It comes from our Mother Earth and is of the Goddess. In addition to this, specific foods have their own inherent powers that can be used and directed towards specific magickal goals. It is important to remember though, that it is the personal power or magick of the witch in her intentions, enchantments that can release and direct these energies to their magickal goals. What a team!

Tomatoes are also called love apples, and indeed they do have the power to induce feelings of romantic love. No wonder the people of Mediterranean countries have the reputation of being romantic, their diets are heavy on the tomato, which also goes extremely well with Basil, an herb associated with love. Need I say more? Garlic of course is protective, so when including garlic in any recipe, visualise it protecting those that are to eat the finished meal and the same is true of its healing properties.

No time for home made herbal oils and teas? Your local store has a wondrous variety of oils now, such as chilli oil, basil oil and lemon oil etcetera. Want to attract extra money to pay an unexpected bill? Drizzle your salad with basil oil, visualise the bill being paid and chant your rhyme before serving the dish.

Old phrases and sayings also give clues as to the inherent magick in certain foods, like 'sowing his oats', 'the apple of his eye' etcetera.

Every time you enter the magickal domain of the kitchen try to feel its inherent nurturing energies. When preparing food, even if there is no specific magickal purpose or intention, practice visualisation of the recipients' pleasure, health and well-being. Pretty soon it will become second nature and you'll be wielding the magick spoons with intent and purpose for health, wealth, harmony and happiness to the benefit of all your family and friends.

Every witch's kitchen should have its own altar. A place where a candle can burn to honour and invoke the Goddess into what is surely sacred space, be it the top of the fridge, a windowsill, or a shelf. Light the candle to the Goddess whenever you are preparing food or working magick of any kind to ensure her presence and blessing throughout. Hestia is the Goddess of the Hearth, so why not dedicate your kitchen to her.

Whether your kitchen is cosy and old-fashioned, country style, clean-lined and clinical, modern or rustic, it is a place where magick is at its fullest potential. Kitchen lore and rites abound and from the earliest of times, the magick of food and healing have gone alongside each other from the open stick fire in a cave, the bubbling cauldron over the cottage hearth, to the modern kitchens of today, witches have worked their magick in these sacred places.

Strings of garlic hanging in the kitchen give protection to the home and its occupants, strings of drying red chillies ensure your relationships remain passionate and they bring warmth to the home. Visualise their purpose as you hang them, and enchant them with rhymes, perhaps something along the lines of 'Garlic, garlic work your will, Keep at bay all that would do ill, or, 'Chilli hot, chilli red, keep fun and passion in my bed'.

The oven has evolved over time from a hollow mound of earth to the characterless objects in our kitchens today but this doesn't mean that the magick is any less powerful. The oven's magick is that of transformation. Being associated with fire, it produces heat to transform raw ingredients into palatable food and useable energy just as it did for the witch of old who stirred her cauldron over an open fire. Microwave ovens produce heat in a different way, but heat is heat and associated with fire, therefore don't knock it; use it. Its magickal energy is just as valid.

Trivets made of wrought iron patterns are collectable magickal items. Having three legs, they are protective and are associated with Moon magic, the law of return, and every Holy Trinity. The patterns on trivets are traditional; I have one with hearts for love, one with flowers, symbolic of freedom and growth and have seen some with pentagrams, birds and even brooms.

Never allow yourself to run out of salt or your money will go too. I keep an unopened pack right at the very back of my highest and most awkward cupboard, that way I don't open it and so I can't run out of it. Salt has always been looked upon as a precious commodity, our word 'salary' is derived from it, and in times past it was not unusual for people to be paid in salt ('worth his salt'?)

A small jar with whisky and seaweed inside, topped with a pound coin and placed on your kitchen windowsill will keep the prosperity coming into your home.

If you have a wood burning or coal burning range and it goes out due to leaving it unattended, place an offering outside your kitchen door to the fire elementals by way of apology or it will be difficult to relight.

Here in Wales, it is traditional to keep good luck and love in the home by hanging a carved love spoon somewhere in the kitchen.

I recently saw a painted ceramic tile in a gift shop that said 'Kitchen Closed'. It may as well have said 'Temple Closed' or 'Heart Closed' in my opinion, for even the busiest Mum or Witch will always keep her kitchen open ready for anything, for who knows when that magick will be needed, and maybe in a hurry.

Offerings of food have been made to the oldest of Gods and Goddesses at important ceremonies and rites of passage since the dawn of time. Tombs in Egypt have been found to contain such offerings and also items of food, magickally charged, to nourish the soul in the afterlife.

All important festivals, sacred and secular, in all cultures are celebrated with feasting and sacred food, such as Yule Logs, Christmas Dinners, Wakes, Birthday Cakes and so on. These are ideal times to bring out the magick in foods, either in decoration, garnishes or the main body of the food. Decorating Yule Cakes (Christmas Cakes) with holly and pentagrams brings the magick of the season and your own personal magick into play. A pie crust embellished with a healing rune, made for someone who is recovering from an illness will speed their recovery.

Brews and potions are made in the kitchen, for healing, love, protection, in fact for any purpose you can imagine. The image of the haggard witch bent over her cauldron of foul smelling evil ingredients is well known. Think of the three witches from Mr. Shakespeare's masterpiece, Macbeth. Thanks, Will. Tongue of Dog? What's that all about? I'll tell you. Many of our common herbs have folk names that are to say the least, colourful. Hound's Tongue is a common wayside herb used for soothing and relieving pain, it is sometimes known as Deer's Tongue. Elf's Wing is Lavender and Graveyard Dust, despite the images the name conjures up, is simply Patchouli Leaves.

Herbal infusions or teas are easy to make and take no time at all. As a general rule of thumb, one ounce of dried herb to a pint of boiling water, or 1 tsp to 1 cup of water infused for five minutes will make an effective remedy or magick brew. Please be careful with the herbs that you use. ALWAYS check with a reputable herbal textbook if you are not sure about the safety of an herb. Generally, very generally, the culinary herbs are safe to use as infusions or teas for internal use. Basil tea will perk you up and properly visualised or enchanted will attract good fortune and cash your way. Rose petals will attract love. Lavender will attract peace. Both of these can be mixed with China tea to produce a magickal brew for these purposes.

**Tea and Tea Leaves**

Let's not forget the good old cuppa. Tea itself has potent energies with the ability to instill courage and stimulate the conscious mind. It has an uplifting quality, not for nothing is it referred to as 'the cup that cheers' and the reputation of being the answer to every problem known to man. Regardless of what ills befell us, my grandmother would bustle about with the kettle and teapot and say 'Never mind, we'll have a nice cup of tea'. It worked too. Tea contains high levels of caffeine, which is a drug, and as with all drugs, constant use can have detrimental and addictive effects, making it's potential for magick considerably less.

The teapot is a magickal tool no less potent than the cauldron or wand. Its shape is receptive and therefore associated with the Goddess, whilst its spout is undeniably male and so is

**124**

associated with the God. The spout and pot combined in the one vessel represent the mystical union of the divine. I have always believed you have to make a fuss of a cup of tea, and will have nothing to do with the modern trend of making tea in the cup. It takes the ritual away from the process and the opportunity to invoke the Goddess and God into blessing the tea. The teapot stand I use is a terracotta disc painted with a pentagram. Sound familiar? My kitchen table doubles as a secondary altar, being the place where I prepare and serve the magickal food I prepare with love for my family and friends, so why not sit the teapot on a Pentacle? The tea cosy I made is embroidered with a Pentagram on one side and on the other 'Blessed Be'. I can't possibly make a cup of tea without doing it magickally!

Turn the teapot clockwise three times for good luck before pouring the first cup.

Reading the tea leaves is fun and an effective magickal use of tea, though Tetley Teabags won't do it, good loose tea is essential. Don't use a strainer to pour the tea and leave the last few drops in the bottom of the cup. Turn it upside down on the saucer and turn it clockwise three times. A rhyme at this point is useful, something like, 'Blessed leaves of sacred tea, show the future now to me'. Pick up the cup and look at the patterns that the leaves have formed on the side of the cup. They will have formed symbols and patterns that can be interpreted by their form or act as a psychic link between the drinker and the reader. Like all forms of divination the tea leaves will act as a trigger to the psychic mind, though some meanings will be obvious such as pound or dollar signs, birds and boats mean travel, fish symbolise the emotions, an arrow shows progress or lack of it by its direction, up meaning good progress, down means the opposite. The nearer to the rim of the cup, the near future is indicated. There are many fine books on the subject, so try it and if you enjoy this relaxing method of divination, learn more.

## Kitchen Tools

Don't be afraid to utilise modern equipment in your magick. The food processor can be as good as the pestle and mortar. I know that the hand grinding infuses ingredients with your own energies, but if you don't have time for that, the processor is better than not working the magick at all. Coffee grinders are excellent at reducing wood chips to a fine powder. This takes forever in the pestle and mortar and is nigh on impossible. The good old coffee grinder does it in minutes and makes the best basis for homemade incense I know, especially if you use apple wood or cedar wood.

Cauldrons have given way to shiny stainless steel pots and pans, but these too are no less magickal. Our practical friend and benefactor, the cottage witch would most certainly have used these items had they been available, she was no mug.

Stir your pots and pans, and cauldrons if you have them, in a clockwise direction to imbue them with positive energies.

Aprons and oven gloves have a mundane protective role so why not use them in protective rituals? Using an oven glove to move a pot of simmering protective potion makes sense physically but visualise them protecting you too and ensure that you put the pot down onto a trivet if you have one. All these tiny elements come together to form the whole of the spell with no extra effort on your part.

# Love Pasta

## Marinara Sauce

2 lbs fresh tomatoes (beef or plum)
1 tbsp extra virgin olive oil
4 ounces chopped onions
2 cloves garlic
2 tbsp tomato puree
Handful torn basil leaves
2 fl oz red wine.
Pinch of sea salt and freshly ground black pepper
1 bay leaf
1 tsp oregano


Spaghetti fresh or dried – enough for two.


Light a pink candle and acknowledge the Goddess. Hestia, She is your kitchen's patron Goddess and perhaps Venus too for the love aspect of the spell.

Peel and de-seed the tomatoes. Take your white handled knife and chop them whilst visualising the one you love who will share this meal with you. If there is no one special in your life right then, visualise yourself in a warm and happy, loving relationship. You'll be amazed how soon that will happen. Enchant the tomatoes with a rhyme.

*'Love for me I soon will see'* or if you are already in a happy marriage or relationship, something like *'Love apples red, ripe and juicy strengthen the bond for my love and me.* Put the tomatoes on one side.

Heat the olive oil in a saucepan on a medium heat or flame, if you have a red pan all the better but it doesn't matter if not. Visualise the love energies in the olives doing their work, feel the warmth of the Mediterranean sun and the Latin romance. Add the chopped onions and garlic. Both of these ingredients have protective energy. See them at work protecting your loved one and your relationship. Cook these until tender and translucent but not brown.

Stir in the tomatoes in a clockwise direction, repeat the rhyme and see the love between you and your partner or future lover.

Add the oregano. This has a peaceful energy, so visualise peace and harmony in your loving relationship.

Add the salt. Salt has long been seen as a blessing, so as you add this ingredient ask the Goddess to bless your love.

Add the ground black pepper. Pepper adds heat and passion to the dish.

Add the bay leaf. One of its magickal properties is protection, so as you add it ask the Goddess to protect your lover.

Turn down the heat and allow the whole to simmer for about 20 mins. If you have a CD player or tape player in the kitchen, play some romantic music whilst it cooks away.

Stir in the red wine, clockwise and allow the sauce to simmer for another 30 mins on a gentle heat until it is of a thick consistency.

During this last 30 mins put a large pan of water on the stove to boil. Add a pinch of salt. Water is the element of love and emotions so ask the water elementals to add their energy to the dish. Visualise protection for your relationship.

Add the spaghetti. Pasta made from wheat is also food of love. Wheat has a high love vibration.

Basil should always be torn rather than chopped and should be added at the very last moments of cooking or it becomes bitter. Basil has strong love energy as well as its influence on finances, so is another appropriate herb in this love magick. See the Basil working its love into the sauce.

Give everything a final stir, clockwise of course. Repeat the original rhyme or come up with something suitable for the whole, such as 'Food of Venus bring love to us. Food of love blessed from above, seal our kiss with magick bliss.'

Drain the pasta and place in a large bowl. Spoon over the Marinara sauce. Bowls are receptive remember and associated with the Goddess, so ask her to bless the food with love before serving.

Light a pink candle on the table and serve the food in the one bowl for you to share.

Enjoy.

# Prosperity Curry

Diced pumpkin
Can of drained chick peas
1 chopped onion
2 cloves of garlic crushed or finely chopped
$1\frac{1}{2}$ tsp ground coriander
$1\frac{1}{2}$ tsp ground cumin
$1\frac{1}{2}$ tsp ground ginger or 1" of fresh ginger, finely chopped
$\frac{1}{2}$ tsp ground cinnamon
4 cloves
2 bay leaves
$\frac{1}{2}$ tsp turmeric
2 heaped tsp mild curry powder
Small carton of plain yoghurt
1 tbsp sunflower oil
Skimmed milk
1 teacup of rice.

Light a green candle, engraved with pound signs or dollar signs if you are 'across the pond', dressed with Basil oil. Invoke your patron Goddess.

In a heavy based saucepan, if you have a green one, use it, if not, no matter, heat the sunflower oil. Sunflowers bring success so this first ingredient will ensure success to your spell. Not a bad way to start!

Add the onion and garlic and cook until tender and translucent. Onions and garlic are protective, visualise protection from negative influences whilst your toss these around the pan.

Add the diced sweet potatoes and the can of chick peas, stir in a clockwise motion. Sweet potatoes have money attracting energy, so as you stir them visualise them bring the necessary cash into your life. Enchant them with a rhyme. *'Potatoes sweet, my needs will meet.'*

Add the spices and stir clockwise and cook for several minutes.

Add the carton of natural yoghurt and stir in. Yoghurt is traditionally an offering to the Goddess, as is all dairy food, and is also an aid to stronger spirituality, which is possibly a good idea in a spell for prosperity as it keeps us from becoming too 'material'.

Allow this cook down for a few minutes then add the skimmed milk. Turn down the heat and simmer gently, stirring occasionally. Each time the curry is stirred, visualise prosperity coming to you and say *'Prosperity come this way, prosperity come to stay'.*

Put the rice into a large pan and cover with exactly double the volume of water. Rice is associated with money and prosperity, so will add to the strength of this wealth spell. Bring the water to the boil and cover the pan immediately with a tight fitting lid. Turn the flame down low and allow the rice to cook until all of the water has been absorbed by the rice. Remove from the heat and allow to stand for several minutes. The rice will continue to absorb the steam inside the pan and the rice grains will stay separate and fluffy.

As you serve the curry and rice onto individual plates enchant the whole dish with a simple rhyme, such as *'Food and spices, rich and hot, simmered in my magick pot, bring cash to see my bills all paid, the wherewithal to see debts laid.'*

# Protective Leek Soup

1 tbsp sunflower oil
4 leeks – roughly chopped
3 potatoes - diced
1 chopped onion
2 cloves garlic
2 bay leaves
1 pint vegetable stock
Salt
Black Pepper

Heat the sunflower oil in a large heavy based saucepan. If you have a copper pan, so much the better, as copper is a protective metal.

Add the onions and garlic, both very protective, and cook until they are tender and translucent. Visualise a cloak of protection forming around you and your family.

Add the diced potatoes and chopped leeks and cook for several minutes. Potatoes are protective in nature as are leeks. Enchant the soup at this stage. *'Protection, protection, come from this broth, effective as a cloak of magick cloth.'*

Add the vegetable stock, black pepper and salt, and bay leaves. Allow to simmer gently for 40 mins stirring occasionally. Each time you stir, clockwise, of course, repeat the enchantment of protection.

# Healing Apple Pie

6 oz wholewheat flour

3 oz butter

1 oz soft brown sugar

4 desert apples peeled and sliced

golden granulated castor sugar

Eggcup of milk for top

Make the sweet pastry, by rubbing in the butter to the flour until it resembles breadcrumbs. Butter is a dairy product and therefore is associated with the Goddess. Ask her to imbue your pie with healing energy. Wholewheat flour has its own healing properties so you are already ahead in the game.

Stir in the ounce of soft brown sugar. Sugar is associated with love and that surely is the energy you need for any healing spell or ritual.

Add sufficient water (I would use spring water or bottled still water for a healing recipe) to form a pliable dough. As you blend the pastry crumbs and water visualise the sick person smiling and well. Place the dough into clingfilm or a plastic bag and place into the fridge to rest for about 20 minutes. As you do this, visualise the recipient of the healing resting too, we all need rest whilst we are sick before we can heal properly.

Divide the pastry into two, approximately into a one third/two thirds ratio and roll out into two circles. The circle is a sacred shape representing the circle of life, see the circles whole and unbroken.

Line a pie dish with the larger of the two pastry subjects and fill with the apples, seeing and feeling the healing energy in the apples. Sprinkle with a small amount of golden granulated sugar. Enchant the pie with a rhyme, like *'Apple sweet, apple sharp, Goddess with your healing harp, return good health to \*\*\*\*\*\*\* for me, as I do will, so mote it be.'*

Cover with the top layer of pastry and seal the edges. As you do this know that you are sealing the spell. Trim off the excess pastry from around the edges of the dish.

Brush the top of the pie with a small amount of milk. Milk is sacred to the Goddess so invoke her aid in the healing spell at this point.

Take the trimmed off pieces of pastry and roll out. Cut out a symbol of healing such as or any sign or symbol that means 'healing' to you.

Bake the pie in a medium hot oven, around $180^0$ C. Remember that the oven is a kitchen tool of transformation. Visualise the transformation of the sick person back into a state of health.

Serve the pie with love to whoever is sick and visualise their health returning with each mouthful.

# Peace and Happiness Pizza

Wholewheat Pizza Dough.

$^{1}/_{4}$ oz of dried fast action yeast

1 tsp golden granulated sugar

9 fl oz hand hot water

1 tsp salt

1 tbsp olive oil


Topping.

14 oz can tomatoes

1 yellow bell pepper

1 red bell pepper

2 cloves garlic

handful of basil leaves

1 tsp dried basil

1 tsp dried oregano

1 tbsp olive oil

2 tbsp tomato puree

$3^{1}/_{2}$ oz Mozzarella cheese

2 tbsp fresh grated Parmesan cheese

Salt and Pepper


## Pizza Dough

Place the yeast and the sugar in a measuring jug with 2 fl oz of the water, leave in a warm place to become frothy, approx 15 mins. The action of the yeast and sugar with the water produces bubbles and froth, symbolic of 'bubbling over' with happiness.

Mix the flour with the salt. Wholewheat flour for the best of health, and wheat has harmonious energies not having been 'molested' and robbed of its vitamins and bran etcetera. Salt is added as a blessing. Visualise the gathered company laughing and healthy, in a harmonious circle around the table.

Make a well in the centre of the flour and add the oil and the yeast mixture with the remaining water. Visualise the addition of the bubbly frothy energy of the yeast mixture, the warmth of the water and the olive oil speaks of glorious Mediterranean sunshine, the very essence of happiness.

This is where you get you hands stuck in there! Get down and get messy, gently mix with your fingers, close your eyes and visualise happiness just pouring from your fingertips into the pizza dough. Mix until the whole mixture leaves the sides of the bowl clean.

Turn the dough out onto a floured board or table top and knead for 4-5 minutes until it is no longer sticky but 'elastic' in nature.

Return it to the bowl and cover with oiled clingfilm and leave to rise for about 30 minutes or until it is doubled in size. Enchant the dough with a rhyme whilst it is rising. Something like *'Bubble and rise, pizza dough, Along with you happiness grow.'*

When risen to twice its original size remove it from the bowl and knead it again for a couple of minutes. Stretch the dough out onto an oiled baking sheet, pushing it out into an even shape. As you stretch and push the elastic dough, visualise your happiness growing and expanding. Do not stretch the dough out to more than $1/2$ inch thick as it will rise again during the baking process.

## Topping

Place the tomatoes, garlic, dried basil and oregano, olive oil and salt and pepper into a saucepan, copper if you have one, as copper is reminiscent of sunshine and therefore happiness. Tomatoes have all encompassing energies, health, wealth, protection and love. With all that lot, who could fail to be happy?? Garlic is protective and health giving, again adding to happiness. Basil and oregano have very positive happiness energy as does the olive. Bring this mixture to the boil, then turn down the heat and allow it to simmer gently until it is reduced and thick. Stir occasionally in a clockwise direction, as you do so visualise happiness and sunshine. Enchant the topping as it cooks down, with a rhyme such as *'Tomatoes and herbs of sunshine bright, bring bubbling happiness to me tonight.'*

After the mixture has thickened, allow it to cool slightly.

Spread the mixture evenly over the top of the dough stopping short about $^1/_2$ inch from the edge of the dough.

Cut the tops from the bell peppers and remove the pith and the seeds. Slice into rings. Place the largest ring from the yellow pepper into the centre of the pizza to represent the sun. Cut the remaining circles in half into curves, arrange around the 'sun' to make rays of sunshine. A rhyme of enchantment here is cool, *'Rays of warmth and summer sun, bring to us happiness and fun.'*

Top with the Mozzarella and Parmesan cheese, dairy products associated with the Goddess and both from Sunny Italy. Bake in the centre of a hot oven, around 200ºC

Serve the pizza to friends and family to bring happiness to them.

# Teas and Brews

### Herbal Teas or Infusions

1 tsp herb to 1 cup of boiling water is the average 'recipe' for an herbal tea. Make the infusion in a teapot and use a strainer, otherwise there will be mouthfuls of bitter herbs. For acute conditions such as colds or 'flu take 6 cups a day for the first 2 days, then reduce to 3 cups a day. For long term use, 3 cups a day is considered the 'safe' dose.

**NEVER TREAT ILLNESS WITH HOME REMEDIES ALONE, SEEK PROFESSIONAL HELP IF ANY CONDITION LASTS MORE THAN A COUPLE OF DAYS.**

### Cold and 'Flu Tea
Equal quantities of Elderflower, peppermint and yarrow is an excellent infusion for colds. Take 3 – 6 cups a day. Add ginger or cayenne if the body is chilled. Add camomile of there is an inability to sleep.

### 'Flu
Influenza is caused by a viral infection which can cause debility and depression if left untreated. Echinacea will build up the immune system and assist in fighting the virus.

### Headaches
Stress headaches respond well to camomile tea but headaches linked to a stomach upset are best treated with an infusion of Rosemary. Feverfew is specific for migraine headache.

**Eczema**
This dry, itchy skin condition can be treated with an herbal infusion allowed to cool and used as a lotion. A strong infusion ( 2 – 4 tsp herb to 1 cup water) of marigold or camomile.

An excellent tea to aid in the treatment of eczema is made from equal parts of dandelion root, burdock root and red clover flowers.

**Hangover**
Never mind 'hair of the dog', drink pints of water to rehydrate the body. Ginger and camomile tea with a squeeze of lemon plus a tsp honey will relieve nausea and headache.

**Indigestion**
Fennel and peppermint tea drunk after meals or when feeling bloated is an excellent remedy for indigestion.

So, you get the general idea? Use food and herbal ingredients that possess the appropriate energies, combine them with visualisation of the outcome of the spell, enchant them with rhyme and prepare them with love.

Get witchin' in that kitchen!

# 12. Hocus Pocus and Eye of Newt

*Cast your spell wherever you will*
*Remember though, for good not ill*
*Cauldron bubble and fire burn*
*Bad luck or curse now will turn*
*Sickness vanish out of sight*
*Bring an end to any plight*
*Need some cash that bill to pay?*
*Extra funds your debts to lay?*
*A lover now into your life?*
*The end result to be a wife?*
*Cast the spell into the night*
*Weave magick for a future bright.*

## Herb magick

Herbs can be used in magick in a variety of ways. Each one is no less effective than the rest but each has its own charm.

## Incense

Incense has been used in magick since the earliest cultures. Remains of incense have been found in Egyptian tombs, Incan pyramids and Stone Age burial sites.

There are three main types of incense, sticks (joss sticks), cones, and loose incense. The loose variety is the easiest and quickest to make so we will concentrate on that form. Once the incense is blended you will require some charcoal discs and a metal or earthenware dish or small pot to burn it in. If this is going to rest on a precious or flammable surface, half fill the pot with earth or sand to absorb the heat. Any pot that will withstand the heat of the burning charcoal block is fine. The charcoal discs are specially prepared to burn at a very high temperature and light very easily. They can be found in occult supply stores, aromatherapy supply stores (these are popping up all over the place right now) or even some health food shops. I have included a list of mail order suppliers at the end of this book.

Herbs and resins are ground into a powder, blended together and burned or smouldered as offerings, requests (petitions), spells or in honour of any of the Gods and Goddesses, or for specific ceremonies or rituals such as the eight Sabbats.

The simple act of grinding the herbs down can become almost meditative and as with all other magick, the intention and direction of the spell is important. Keep the purpose of the incense firmly in your mind whilst you grind the ingredients down. Enchant the herbs individually if you wish or collectively as you blend them together.

Light the charcoal block and allow it to become white-hot. Sprinkle on a teaspoon of incense and visualise your spell in the swirling, curling fragrant smoke. Depending on your environment, you may wish to have a window slightly open as the smoke from burning incense can sometimes be quite overpowering. Hacking and coughing does somehow manage to diminish the magick!

Resins such as Frankincense and Myrrh are very hard to reduce to a fine powder and become very sticky and gooey the more you grind them, so larger crystals are fine here. Wait 'til you see the pestle and mortar!

Don't grind resins or plant materials that may have a toxic effect in the same pestle and mortar that you use for cooking purposes. Okay, I know you wouldn't, but I said it anyway. Once the herbs and other ingredients are ground and ready, mix them together in a large bowl. Use your magick fingers and infuse them with your magickal goal. If you haven't enchanted the individual ingredients with a rhyme, definitely do it now.

There are many brilliant books on the market that give almost endless listings and correspondences for herbs and their purposes that I will add to the end of this book. Meanwhile, I have included a short list in End Bits. At first, look for herbs that are multi-purpose, so that your initial purchases or pickings are minimal. You will expand your herb cupboard as you get more confident in the art.

**Oils**

Essential oils are so easy to obtain now but ensure that you buy pure oils, as many of the so-called aromatherapy oils on the market are synthetic. Whilst they are fine if they are all you can get, there is definitely more magick in the pure oils.

These wonderfully fragrant oils can be added to incense blends, or heated in an oil burner, filling your space with magickal fragrance. In an oil burner, top the cup part up with water. I always use spring, filtered or bottled still water for this, as both are free of impurities. Do you really want fluoride and chlorine in your spell? Then add a few drops of an appropriate oil or blend of oils. Visualise your magickal purpose and enchant the fragrant liquid as it sends your magick out into the ether.

## Herbal Petitions

On a new piece of paper, write or draw symbols that represent your need. Pound signs, a smiley face, a heart, a shield, whatever. Put a couple of drops of appropriate oil (i.e. basil or patchouli for a money petition, lavender oil for peace and harmony, etc) on your fingertip and rub onto the paper. Choose the right herbs, rose for love, garlic for protection, lavender for peace etcetera. Place the herb in the centre of the piece of paper and screw it up like the blue packets of salt that used to appear in packets of crisps (now you KNOW the crone is upon me!) enchant it and burn it. As the petition burns, 'see' your magickal goal coming into fruition.

## Herbal Pouches

Similar in principle to the herbal petition, except instead of burning the petition, put it into a pouch with a long drawstring and keep it on you, hanging from a belt or a belt loop inside a skirt or pants. This will keep the energy around you in your aura and attract the necessary outcome into manifestation.

## Sympathetic magic

This type of magick works on the principle that like attracts like. Using dolls (Poppets) to represent people, banknotes in a money spell, photographs, symbols, emblems, models the list is endless. For example, a healing spell for a sick friend or family member could incorporate a photograph of that person in a state of happiness and health, placed on your pentacle or plate, surrounded by healing crystals, a healing petition, a light blue (for health) candle and an enchantment in rhyme. This will work on the principle that the healing energies from the light blue candle and the crystals in conjunction with the enchantment will return that person to the state of health in the picture. This is sometimes known as absent healing. Any personal object belonging to the sick friend or relative will also add power to the spell. A word of caution however, even with a healing ritual, it is not strictly ethical to perform magick without the other person's knowledge or consent unless it is an emergency or they cannot be contacted.

**Poppets**

These are very basic rag dolls. A piece of cloth cut into two gingerbread man shapes, stitched together and stuffed. They can be embellished with embroidered faces or hair or even clothing similar to that worn by the object of the spell. Enchant the poppet and tell it who it is to represent. This isn't voodoo or black magick, merely like attracting like energies!

**A spell for the return of a lost pet**

Place a photograph of the straying pet onto the pentacle (plate) on your altar. If it is a cat, an ornament of a cat next to it will be great and so on for any animal. Catnip on the altar adds extra power for the return of a feline wanderer. Use a brown candle (brown is the colour for pets and the home so both in one!) Light the candle and call to the animal. Keep returning to the spell on the altar and calling to the pet.

In the meantime, a bowl of its favourite food by the door and a few phone calls to vets and animal sanctuaries can't hurt, along with a card in the local newsagents. Have your pets microchipped and the results will be even quicker!
Make a fuss of the returning offender.

**144**

## A spell to sell your house

An oil associated with money or business such as basil is needed here. Anoint the For Sale sign in the garden by rubbing the post with the oil. 'Write' on the actual sign SOLD with the oil. A suitable enchantment in rhyme such as 'This house be sold, this house be gone, this house be sold so I can move on.' Tell the house that you have been happy there and will miss it but it's time for you to move on. Thank it for its protection in the past and ask it to be as kind to the new occupiers.

On a copy of the Estate Agents written details of your house, write SOLD in bold letters on the photograph of the property.

This spell also works for buying a property too. Anoint the For Sale sign on the post with your name (if you have the opportunity, but don't get caught trespassing if you can help it!). On the Estate Agents details write in bold letters across the photograph, 'SOLD TO *******' with your name. Toss a tigers eye crystal into the garden in an unobtrusive spot, tell the crystal that you will retrieve it when you move in. It's worked for me every time, even in circumstances where logic insisted that we should not have been able to buy the property for whatever reason. That includes where I live right now.

## For Cash to pay an unexpected bill

Place the bill onto the pentacle. Surround it with crystals that possess money attracting energies such as Green Aventurine, Jade, Peridot, Green tourmaline. Coal works well too. Light a green candle that has been dressed with Patchouli oil and engraved with appropriate symbols etc. Write PAID in bold letters across the bill and rub some Patchouli oil onto it. Sprinkle dried basil or fresh basil leaves over the top. Enchant the whole with a suitable rhyme.

## For Exam Success

A purple candle anointed with Rosemary oil and suitable engraved or charmed. If you have any past papers for the exam place them on the pentacle but write on the top the date of the exam. Take a red pen and draw a giant tick right across the page. Sprinkle dried Rosemary, for concentration, over it and some cinnamon for success. If the spell is for someone else, a photograph of them can be added to the assembly. Enchant the whole thing.

Organised revision and study periods are also necessary!

A similar spell for success in an interview works wonders too. Instead of the exam paper, place a copy of the job advert or something else appropriate to the circumstances. Repeat the above process from there.


## To attract a lover

A pink or red candle, depending on whether you are looking for romantic or sexual love, anointed with rose oil or patchouli, again dependant on which type of love you are seeking.

Take two different coloured threads and tie them in a knot. Place it on the pentacle. Add hearts, and a magnet. Sprinkle with pepper for attracting sexual love, or rose petals for romantic love. Enchant the whole.

NOTE. It is unethical to work these spells for the attraction of particular individuals. This is manipulation and definitely bad mojo! Work the spells in general terms and let your own charms do the rest.

## A Happy Marriage Spell for Newlyweds

Take a piece of pale blue material (the colour of peace and tranquillity) and place on it a silver coin, a piece of coal (if you can find one), a piece of bread, a pinch of salt, a seed, a green crystal, a rose quartz crystal. These will ensure that the couple will continue to enjoy, food on their table, warmth in their home, fertility, health and prosperity and love and harmony. Tie it up with a purple ribbon and ask the Goddess to bless the couple. Enchant the whole thing with a suitable rhyme and give it to the happy couple on their wedding day.

## Car Park Full

This one works for me almost every time. As you approach the car park, visualise a car pulling out of a space right in front of you. Chant *'Elemental powers hark, find for me a place to park.'*

## The Witch's Bottle

This is a spell for protection of your home and all its occupants.

Take a small, pretty bottle or jar with a lid or cork and fill it three quarters full with sewing pins. Visualise the pins piercing any negativity and neutralising it. Fill the rest of the bottle with oddments of different coloured threads. Push them down inside the bottle and allow them to tangle and knot themselves around the pins. This is to tangle any harm and cause it confusion. Put the top on or the cork in the bottle. Light a candle and drip wax around the top to seal the bottle.

Hold the bottle in both hands and send your own energy through your hands into the bottle. Enchant the spell with a rhyme. *'Bottle of pins and tangled thread charm, guard our home and keep it from harm. Curse or bane that enters within, be knotted in thread and pierced with pin.'*

To protect your computer from crashing or a virus

We look to communication for this spell. The crystal associated with Mercury the planet and God of communication is Aventurine. It is also associated with the air element, the element of communication. So, if you have one, place an aventurine crystal on top of the central processing unit and visualise an invisible shield surrounding it. A rhyme of enchantment could be something such as 'Crystal smooth, crystal green, crystal called aventurine, guard my computer day and night, see any virus put to flight. Stop it crashing, keep it live, ensure my data will survive.'

If you don't have an aventurine crystal, a pot of parsley growing next to the computer works just as well. Parsley is an herb of mercury and therefore associated with communication. Enchant the parsley, *'Parsley guard my computer day and night, put every virus out to flight. Stop it crashing, keep it live, ensure my data will survive.'*

## To make your bread rise

As you mix the yeast into your bread dough, visualise a balloon in the shape of a loaf. See it rising high into the air as light as a feather. While the dough is rising, visit it occasionally and enchant it, *'Dough that forms my daily bread, be as a feather and not of lead, reach right up to touch the sky, form a loaf that's light and high.'*

## Car Protection Spell

To keep you safe whilst driving or travelling in your car place a clove of garlic in the glove compartment. Enchant it with a rhyme *'Pungent bulb of strong protection keep me safe from each direction. Wherever I travel be my charm keep this car safe from harm.'*

## Lou's Cholesterol Spell

To help lower your cholesterol levels (in conjunction with a sensible diet!). Take a block of lard and cut a portion off it each day. Place the cut portion in a pan and melt it. Dig a small hole in your garden or make a hole in some soil in a plant pot. Pour in the melted lard and cover again with soil whilst visualising fat cells in your body and bloodstream dissolving and disappearing. Enchant the melted lard with a rhyme like this, *'Harmful fat be melted and gone, to keep me healthy and living long.'*

This one works well for those struggling with sugar. Dissolve a spoonful of sugar into a cup of warm water. Pour the liquid into a vase of cut flowers or a pot plant.

## To Find a Lost Object

Can't find your glasses? Car keys? Here's a simple spell that usually works for me.

Visualise the lost object. Take a pin and a cushion, visualise the object sitting in the centre of the cushion and stick a pin into the cushion (metaphysically 'pinning it down'). Forget about it and within a short time you will either remember where the object is, or simply come across it!

So, you have the idea? Sympathetic magic works by like attracting like. Whenever you work a spell, enchant it with a simple rhyme. An old witches saying is *'If ye would witch's magick make, Be sure the spell in rhyme be spake.'*

So happy witchin', get those spells a brewin'.

# 13. Divination

*Tarot cards and leaves of tea*
*Show to me my destiny.*
*Witch's runes and crystal ball*
*Of my future, reveal all.*

## General Principles

Psychic ability is a gift that we all possess. It's just a matter of getting in touch with that energy and with practice using it to give us a better insight into our lives. Tarot cards, playing cards, runes etcetera, are all the traditional divination tools of the witch, but alone they mean nothing. They are simply triggers for your own psychic mind to come to the fore. Your 'intuition' if you will.

## Tarot cards

The images on a tarot card may have traditional meanings, but at any one time they may 'speak' to you of something different. Whilst it is good to understand the meanings of the tarot in general, it is more important to listen to their whispers to your psychic centre. I have given very basic traditional interpretations of the Tarot and they usually come with a booklet explaining any differences from the original designs, but this won't replace 'getting to know' your cards.

There are many different packs available quite inexpensively at the moment, something to suit all tastes and interests, but in the beginning I think it is important to understand and know the traditional designs such as the Ryder Waite pack or The Tarot of The Old Path. Having said that, adhering to the principle that whatever feels right to you is good. If you feel 'in tune' with any of the multitude out there, then go for it. You will develop 'a feel' for a pack and it will be personal. In my case, when I look at a new tarot pack, if I feel at home with the High Priestess and the Hermit, then I know I can work with that pack. The indicator for you will be different, but there are usually one or two cards that you will have a special affinity with.

Once you have chosen and purchased your tarot pack, bless them and consecrate them just as you did your other tools, for tools they are. Spend some time just shuffling through and absorbing the images that face you. Sleep with them under your pillow for a couple of nights. When not being used keep them wrapped in a silk scarf or other piece of material, this will prevent them from absorbing everyday energy. I keep mine in a beaded velvet pouch. The old rule goes, whatever seems right to you.

The tarot pack is divided into two parts, the major arcana and the minor arcana. The 22 cards of major arcana are the court cards, like the picture cards of any playing deck and the 40 cards of the minor arcana are numbered cards that are divided into four suits, pentacles, wands, cups and swords. Each of these divisions is aligned to an element; pentacles are associated with earth and finances, cups with water and emotions, swords with air and thought patterns and wands with fire and the work environment and transformations.

The major arcana or court cards are associated with people that touch our lives, including us, and are useful in exploring our relationships. These cards are also numbered beginning at 0 to 21. These cards represent our journey through life and events that take place and affect us deeply.

When reading the tarot, there are both positive and negative aspects to their meanings and messages. Traditionally and for beginners, look for the negative aspect of a card when it appears reversed in a spread.


## The Major Arcana

### 0. *The Fool*
In traditional packs, the fool is represented by a young man dressed as a jester and depicted about to step off the edge of a cliff into the unknown. There is usually a small dog biting at his ankles or clothing. The fool isn't falling so it appears that he is taking a deliberate step. The dog represents inner knowing and intuition so tells us that the Fool, although stepping out into the unknown on the beginning of a journey, either physical or spiritual, has an intuitive knowledge of what he is doing. This card tells of new beginnings and a need to trust in our inner voice of intuition.

Negatively, the Fool is telling us to watch our step, that danger is but a step away.


### 1. *The Magician*
He is Merlin of Arthurian legend, a trickster, the wizard in the fairy tale. He is a bringer about of change, a manipulator of energies. The magician is usually depicted in front of his altar that bears a wand, a sword, a pentacle and a cup. Sound familiar? His working tools also represent the four elements of the minor arcana that together create the fifth element, spirit, which brings about our desires and necessary changes. The magician uses the strength of his will to bring about change along with his understanding of the elements and their place in our world and in magic. This card tells us that we are required to use our own strengths and talents in a given situation or when we are seeking answers or change.

Negatively, the Magician warns us against manipulation of others rather than using our own talents to achieve a desire or goal.

### 2. *The High Priestess*
This Lady is depicted seated on a throne between a black and white pillar. She is the High Priestess of the sacred temple and the guardian of its secrets, and is representative of the Goddess in her maiden aspect. The moon is usually present and often in its crescent form speaking to us of the Maiden. She asks us to explore our spiritual or psychic aspects and to make time to connect to the Goddess, however busy we may seem.

If there is a negative aspect to this card, it is in that she can become detached and aloof in her relationships with others.

### 3. *The Empress*
This Lady is strong, usually depicted as pregnant, for she is the Goddess in her Mother aspect. She is the Good Fairy, and brings fertility and abundance in whatever aspect we are seeking guidance. She is creativity in its purest form.

The Empress brings life and fertility to any projects that we are about to undertake and usually is an assurance of success, especially if the project involves payment or recognition.

Negatively, the Empress can warn of love turning to a form of martyrdom, or a smothering, possessive love.

### 4. *The Emperor*
He is the King, the wealthy and earthly representative of stability and power. He is sometimes depicted dressed ready for battle because he is courageous and assertive. He brings

power to our desires and assists in bringing the material needs into being. He often gives us the necessary courage and assertiveness to help ourselves.

The Emperor in his negative guise can warn us of the intervention of a selfish or miserly man into our affairs.

### 5. *The High Priest*
Sitting on a spiritual throne, he is the male counterpart of the Goddess as the High Priestess. He is the wielder of spiritual wisdom and gives us access to our own spirituality. He tells us to listen to our Higher Self, the part of ourselves that is in contact with the divine.

In his negative aspect, the High Priest can be quite terrifying. He tells us of an inclination to turn to dark powers to achieve our goals and ambitions. He can also warn of a tendency to harbour guilt feelings from the past disallowing us to move on spiritually or emotionally.

### 6. *The Lovers*
This card invariably depicts a pair of naked lovers. It represents duality in relationships, love and also our relationship with ourselves. It often represents a choice to be made between two paths. It may speak of new relationships or a new aspect of an existing relationship. It usually tells us to come to a decision over any issue that we have been dithering over.

Negatively, the Lovers speak to us of a conflict in priorities or needs, confusing the issue and preventing us to come to a decision in an important matter.

### 7. *The Chariot*

The charioteer is driving the chariot hard, pulled by a black and a white horse. It is the card of travel, of direction or positive movement. It is the card of overcoming obstacles that may lie in your path. This card means movement, possibly out of a period of stagnation, it may mean physical or emotional movement.

The negative side of the Chariot warns us of any tendency to ride rough shod over others. It can indicate that we are unable to face a situation that stems from deep inside, preferring to move the situation to disguise it, when what we really need to do is to make the changes inside first before progress can take place.

### 8. *Strength*

Traditionally, the Strength card depicts a female holding open the very toothy mouth of a lion. It is the card of inner strength, mind over matter. Strength that comes from an unexpected source is associated with this card. It can indicate the strength of repeated effort to solve a problem or solving it with intelligence or gentle energy rather than brute force.

If there is a negative aspect to the Strength card it lies in a possible refusal to tackle a problem creatively rather than with aggression.

### 9. *The Hermit*

This is the card of the still small voice of inner wisdom, our Higher Self, the part of us that knows the answers from the divine instinctively. He holds a lantern representing our own inner light. This card tells us that in times of trouble or in seeking answers to major problems it is necessary to seek our own counsel in the matter. He represents our unconscious mind and ancient collective wisdom. It can tell us that we need to have some quality quiet time, to walk in nature, or to meditate and just 'be' with ourselves.

Negatively, the Hermit warns of being too dependent on others or a tendency to ignore pressing matters, sweep them under the carpet in the hope they will disappear. They won't folks!


### 10. *The Wheel of Fortune*

The roulette wheel of the tarot. Spin the wheel, where will it fall? The Wheel of Fortune is usually spun by the blindfolded Goddess, Fortuna. Riding on the wheel are a variety of strange creatures, very often one of them is a sphinx. This card hints at a possibility of fate having a hand in the affairs of mankind, an overseeing by deities or 'powers that be'. This is so to a certain extent, but mankind are the most fortunate, or maybe unfortunate of species, in that we are given a conscious choice in the handling of our lives and decisions which really means that it is us in control of our lives and destinies. The old Wheel of Fortune is spinning though, and this card does indicate that a change in fortune is on the way, for good or bad. Positive or negative may be as simple as whether or not the card is reversed in the spread or not. Just by a spin of this wheel, our lives can change overnight.

This card can act as a psychic alarm bell, warning of imminent change and allow us to take a step back and see things more clearly, perhaps taking steps to prevent a forthcoming disaster, or in its positive aspect to go out and meet good fortune half way.

Negatively, the Wheel of Fortune warns us not to allow a fortune-teller or other person who has an influence on us to give us a 'laid down in stone' picture of the future. Our futures change constantly and we can change them instantly by a single action or reaction.

## 11. *Justice*

The figure on this card is probably a familiar sight of a female figure holding aloft the sword and scales of justice. This figure can be seen outside many a courthouse, notably, the Old Bailey.

This card is traditionally associated with the law and other official matters. It can represent a legal contract aspect of a new job or sale, even a court case. More generally it represents good principles and standards, high ideals.
Negatively, Justice warns us of falling foul of the law, or the fact that we may become victims of injustice. It may indicate a failed law-suit.

## 12. *The Hanged Man*

He hangs by one leg upside down from the World Tree. This is the card of suspension, of marking time or delays. It can also be interpreted as the card of self-sacrifice. This sacrifice can be noble or not dependent upon motive. Self-sacrifice in the name of martyrdom is most definitely bad mojo guys and not the interpretation of the positive aspect of this card.

Negative aspects of this card warn of the martyrdom scenario above. It can warn us against impulsiveness and impatience.

## 13. *Death*

The Grim Reaper. The grinning skull of the skeleton with the cloak and scythe usually brings the same reaction from the novice. Oh, oh. The Death Card, now what? Get out the insurance policies? Let me stress quite categorically right here, that the Death card vary rarely means physical death, unless the surrounding cards also indicate this.

Death is seen as an ending, and that is the traditional meaning of this card. Something is coming to an end.

Remember though, that endings cannot be seen in isolation. Where there is an ending there is also a beginning. That is the nature of things.

Death is a natural change, a time of transition from one state into another and we have to experience many 'little deaths' in life so that we can make progress and move forwards.

Negatively Death warns us of an inability to 'let go', to close a door in order for another to open.

## 14. *Temperance*
In almost any chosen Tarot pack, the Temperance card shows an angelic being pouring water from one vessel into another and the card generally exudes a feeling of peace and harmony. This is the card of balance and equilibrium, keeping our lives on an even keel. Temperance helps us to create our own 'quiet place' inside and asks us to avoid overreaction to adverse conditions and not to make a drama out of a crisis.

On the negative side, Temperance warns us against letting go of reality. She asks us to stand up to what isn't right and not be so laid back that everything goes over our heads.

## 15.*The Devil*
The Devil is another card that sometimes evokes extreme reaction. It isn't a card of impending doom but asks us to acknowledge the dark sides of our natures, to be in touch with our baser instincts and accept ourselves for what we are, warts and all. It is a card of destruction, but destruction is sometimes necessary before creation can take place, giving us a nudge albeit sometimes a hefty one to bring about the impetus for change. Outmoded thinking or negative habits have to be destroyed before a change for the positive can take place.

It's okay to feel homicidal on a bad day, when everything and everyone is pouring negativity over you. It's okay to say 'Hey, buster, back off.' We are humans and we can't be sweetness and light constantly (Thank the Goddess!) The Devil teaches us to let rip when our emotions and feelings are in chaos, for to deny these feelings will cause more harm than remaining Miss or Mr. Perfect. It's okay to cry and it's okay to yell when things get on top of you. Join the club.

Negativity shows itself in Temperance when we are prone to drown in our own negative emotions and wallow in self-pity.

Shout it out, and, make 'em run for cover!


### 16. *The Tower*
The Tower or The Blasted Tower as it is sometimes known is yet another card illustrated with disaster. The tower is struck by lightening and falling apart, there are bodies flying everywhere, looks like a bad day all round. Yet in the Tower we find once more destructive forces put to positive use. The destructive or cleansing energy of the Tower is often swift and unexpected, or it can be forceful and urgent because we have continued to ignore our little warnings and inner voices up to now. We know there has to be change but we just can't be bothered. The Tower says, 'Hey Buddy, you WILL change 'cos I'm gonna make you.' The change that occurs can sometimes look like an obstacle or a setback but usually in time we can see that when the dust has settled, the situation is actually better for this sudden purging.

It's negative aspect warns us not to build anything on a less than firm base, otherwise … yep, collapse is inevitable.

## 17. *The Star*

The Star brings hope. All throughout history in almost every culture we can see this, the Star of Bethlehem, we 'Wish on a Star', we look for our futures 'in the Stars'. The Star of the Tarot lights and guides us on the way to reaching our goals and really can make our dreams come true but whatever we dream of, however old we are, we need to make the initial move to bring the Star's energy into being. This book would never have been written and published if I hadn't bitten the bullet and sat down before my blank computer screen and begun with the words 'To The Cottage Witch, Past and Present.' You have to 'Follow your Star.'

All the Tarot cards have a negative aspect and the Star is no exception and can manifest in not being able to settle for less. It is no good wasting our lives and wishing our lives away if we aren't prepared to do something about it. The Star will always give hope if you can be bothered to get off your tushie.

## 18. *The Moon*

The Moon is the card of spirituality and psychism. It usually portrays two dogs baying at the moon whilst from behind a scorpion is emerging from a pool. This card asks us to live our lives in harmony with nature and with the times and tides of nature. We are asked to live imaginatively and creatively following our instincts and inner voices. Follow your heart and defy logic.

Negatively the Moon warns against over reliance on magick without being prepared to shift your butt to help yourself.

## 19. *The Sun*

The Sun shines and everyone feels better. It is a symbol of all that is positive and energetic. Traditional Tarot designs for the Sun show two children holding hands and playing under the hot midday sun. Anything is possible when the Sun shines and when it appears in your Tarot spread. It represents success and pure joy, of reaching our fullest potential in whatever field we choose to find our challenges.

The negative aspect of the Sun warns against making the mistake of identifying success and attainment as one and the same. Fulfillment doesn't always come from material acquisition and it is sometimes the journey that is more fulfilling than actually reaching the destination.

### 20. *Judgement*
There is an angel blowing a trumpet on traditional designs of this card, and down below people are rising from there graves for the Day of Judgement. This card looks at putting things to rest and making recompense for any of our mistakes. Who makes the judgement? God? The Goddess? No, the final judgement is our own. We need to accept ourselves and our imperfections and acknowledge our place in the Great Scheme of things. Sometimes things from the past cannot be changed or put right. It is time to let those go and file them in The Great Wastepaper Basket. It's okay to let yourself get rid of things we can't reconcile, it's not okay to do it and then go repeat the process over again.

Negatively, Judgement asks us to use our own judgement in situations, follow instincts rather than logic if instinct seems to be the right thing to do.

### 21. *The World*
The Fool's journey is over. He has travelled full circle through challenges and adversities and is now everything he can be. Remember though, that in every ending lies a new beginning. When we dance on this Earth we are always seeking a new step. The World shows us completion but only in completion of

a stage or phase of life, for even in death we are merely in transit to another beginning. This card is one of movement and potential fulfillment. Whatever projects or undertakings we have been involved in are coming to fruition. The World is our oyster.

Yes, even The World has a negative interpretation. Remember that we don't travel on this Earth alone and The World reversed warns us against leaving behind those that we choose to travel with when we are fulfilling our own ambitions and dreams.

## The Minor Arcana

This part of the Tarot is divided into four suits, pentacles, wands, swords and cups. Symbolic of the four elements they also have associations with different aspects of our lives. The Cups speak to us of our loves and emotions, Pentacles speak materially and of our finances, Wands generally refer to our work through life be it paid or unpaid, Swords represent our thoughts and thinking processes.

These cards are numbered from1 to 10 plus the Court Cards, like the picture cards of a deck of playing cards. These cards represent personalities and people that are in our lives or about to put in appearance. They are archetypal figures that bring us insight into those who we share our lives with. The King and Queen of each suit are joined by the Page and Knight, two characters instead of one, the Jack, in a playing card deck.

### Aces

Aces speak of new beginnings and these will be relevant to the ruling suit that belongs to the card. For instance, the Ace of Cups will indicate a new relationship or a new phase in an already exiting relationship, and so on for Wands, where the Ace could mean the opportunity of a new career or maybe a promotion or change in direction of an existing career. The Aces are cards of change.

Negatively, Aces warn us against stagnation and resistance to change.

### Twos
It is the number of partnership, whether in life as a marriage, on business, in co-operation in any project. They speak of duality and steady growth.

Negatively, a two will warn against over-dependence on a partner.

### Threes
One and one makes three. Threes tell us of fruits that are born from a partnership, whether it is a child (three of cups) or a business (wands), threes represent working with others to achieve success. It speaks of initial success in a project that will encourage you to carry on.

On the negative side, threes warn against independence when it isn't appropriate to go it alone.

### Fours
Four square. Fours are the number of organisation and limitations, but remember most of our limitations are self-imposed. Fours speak of keeping hold of reality. Not everything can be perfect and we have to change things according to our lives to be comfortable. Fours assist in this process.

Negatively, fours warn us of a lack of confidence in our abilities and ask us to expand our horizons by removing the barriers we have put up ourselves.

### Fives
Fives are the cards of communication and change. They demand movement in our lives where there is none. They insist that we speak out and be heard.

Negatively fives can indicate a small loss and ring alarm bells warning of malice and gossip.

### Sixes
While fives are in constant motion and herald change, sixes are the cards of stability and firm foundations. They speak of harmony and peace.

Negative aspects of the sixes warn us that perhaps all is not as it seems and we must take a real hard look at what's going on. Maybe, underneath, things 'aint that rosy.

### Sevens
Sevens are the cards of the Moon and speak of spirituality and the unconscious mind. They indicate spiritual achievement rather than the attainment of material possessions. They ask us to seek the Holy Grail, to find the meaning of life.

Negatively they warn against the quick fix situation rather than taking a step back and calmly looking inside ourselves for the reason behind what may be going on for us.

### Eights

Eights speak of acquiring new skills and talents or new situations. Cards of movement, eights tell us not to give up on what can be put right.

The negative aspect of the eights warns against resistance to necessary change.

### Nines

Courage friend. That is the message of the nines. Keep going to the end of the road. It may be tough but you CAN do it. They ask us to rely on our inner strength, because it will see us through. Be yourself and be all that you can be.

Negatively, nines warn against over-dependence on others in any given situation.

### Tens

The last of the numbered cards of the Minor Arcana, tens speak of completion, the end of the journey or task. They herald fulfillment and perfection but remember, after completion comes a new beginning, we are constantly evolving and reaching for new challenges, so don't get too comfy for too long.

The negative face of the tens warns against dissatisfaction and sterility in our achievements. They say 'Hey Bud, Well done. Now get moving and do something else or do something WITH your achievements.'

## The Court Cards

The Court Cards are comprised of Kings, Queens, Knights and Pages. These are representative of personalities and relationships in our lives. Sometimes they can reflect us in any given phase of life.


## Pages

Pages are bringers of news, the heralds. As personalities they are often representative of a young person, child or early teenager.

Negatively, the pages can represent someone who is childish in nature (not childlike).


## Knights

These are the original knights in shining armour. They are off on a quest or crusade and nothing is gonna stop them. He's definitely one of life's free spirits.

Negatively, the Knight warns against going off and doing our own thing and neglecting everyone else and everything else that is important in our lives.


## Queens

Queens are the mature women in our lives, the female authority figures, mothers, grandmothers or older sisters. They 'mother' us, and dependent on the ruling suit show us where we need to cosset ourselves a little.

Negatively though, the Queens show us that we could be becoming possessive about a person or relationship, smothering rather than mothering. It's time to cut those apron stings folks, and kick 'em out into the big bad world. But make sure you're there when they come home with their tales between their legs!

## Kings

Seated in regal spleandour, the Kings rule with authority and wisdom. They are the fathers, the father-figures, the boss or the husband. They have worldly wisdom as opposed to the spiritual wisdom of the Queens.

Negatively, the Kings warn against domineering, overbearing personalities.

So there we have it, the wonderful Tarot. We have made a flying visit into the realm of the cards and I have given you a very brief insight into the interpretation of the cards. Get to know your cards, spend time with them and above all listen to them, they may speak to you of anything but what is normally associated with any particular card. Open your mind and your heart to them and they will be your friends and like a friend will be there for you.

One last thing though, remember that nothing is laid down in stone. The cards show us what is possible or what may happen, we have the power and the choice to change things. Otherwise what would be the point? Tarot helps us to take control of our lives in a constructive and positive way.

Enjoy.

# The Runes

What is a rune? Literally, it is a letter from an ancient alphabet, or a spell in rhyme. Runes in the context of divination however, are small pieces of wood, plain or carved, small ceramic tiles, crystals or evenly sized small pebbles, engraved or painted with runic symbols to aid clairvoyance or open the psychic mind. There are some pretty elaborate (and expensive) rune sets available to buy now, but the best set of runes I have ever possessed is a set I made myself, collecting small pebbles from the edge of a river and painting the runes on with black nail polish, then covering the whole with clear nail polish! This is an area where home-made is best and not only that, easy.

There are several runic alphabets, but the most commonly used for divination purposes are the Norse runes, or the Anglo Saxon runes.

Like the Tarot, divination with runes is a vast subject and probably far better dealt with in a book devoted the subject alone, but I will give a brief overview of the runes and their most basic meanings. If you feel drawn to the runes then I recommend that you invest in such a book, or at least borrow one from a library or very understanding friend (if you go for the latter, please make sure you return it!) The runes are like the Tarot in another way, their interpretation can be negative or positive depending on whether they fall upright or reversed but also read in conjunction with nearby runes to indicate their negativity or not. The exact interpretation is dependant on the question being asked.

### Wyrd

Wyrd (pronounced weird) is the rune of fate. It is a blank rune and should be read in conjunction with the runes that fall close by. This rune can mean all things to all people, it is open to many interpretations and because of this it is the rune that is most likely to open your psychic mind.

### Feoh ᚠ

This is the rune that represents how you earn your living, rewards for hard work or fulfillment. It can indicate a career opportunity that would be of benefit; negatively it may indicate that this is not the time for a career move. Feoh appearing after a grotty time tells us that the sun is about to shine!

Negatively, Feoh warns of a loss of some kind. When Feoh turns up reversed, watch out, something is not quite right.

### Ur ᚢ

Ur is the rune of good health. If it appears after an illness it indicates a speedy recovery. It always indicates strong or wild emotions. It tells of changes that are imminent, of getting rid of unwanted or outdated emotions and physical clutter, this rune appears with regularity around Imbolc and Ostara urging us to get rid of whatever is no longer needed!

The negative side of Ur may indicate failure or a lack of will power, possibly a tendency to allow someone of a stronger nature to assert their influence over you. The rune of change in a negative position means that the changes coming will probably not make you grin.

## Thorn ᚦ

This rune is the rune of protection and luck. In the case of luck it is usually from an unexpected source.

Negative aspects of Thorn can mean the end of a run of good luck. It urges us not to rest on our laurels because, as we know, all things pass, bad and good. It asks us to heed advice that is given rather than plunging headlong into an unwise course of action. Don't make any swift decisions when Thorn is present in a reversed position.

## Os ᚩ

This is the rune of the spoken word, but can also indicate learning or an exam situation. It tells us not fear any situation that we are not truly comfortable with as we will find the right words to see us through. More advice comes through Os, advice given when this rune is present should be heeded, it is kindly and wise advice. In the learning situation a teacher or mentor will be most helpful.

Reversed, Os implies deceit. Don't take everything you hear on face value and advice given is biased in favour of the giver not the receiver.

## Rad ᚱ

Rad is the rune of movement and travel. Physical journeys will be safe and enjoyable, spiritual journeys should be adhered to, you are on the right path. It can also indicate unexpected news.

Rad reversed is generally not good news, literally. It can also indicate that any journey will be enforced rather than chosen and that the outcome may not be what is expected.

***Ken*** ᚲ

Ken is energy, power and strength. It is protective and asks us to open ourselves to good influences that are coming our way. This is a good time to begin new projects or enter new relationships. Ken is the rune of creativity and is especially important to writers, artists and crafts people.

When Ken appears reversed it portends an ending or a loss. It asks us not to hang on to relationships that are over and urges us to delay the beginning of new projects, this is not the time to do it.

***Gifu*** ᚷ

Gifu is a gift. Look at the rune, there is no reversed position for it, it's positive and whichever way you look at it, Gifu really is a gift whether it be a material or emotional or spiritual gift. Gifu will appear when a period of bad luck or bad times has dogged you. It is about to be over.

***Wyn*** ᚹ

Wyn means joy and happiness are coming to you. There will be a positive outcome to anything that you may have been working on. It's your day. It's the sweet smell of success. To the artistic or creative it indicates joy in your work, in this respect it is a perfect partner to Ken.

Wyn reversed should be interpreted as exactly the opposite of its upright meaning. In this position, Wyn can indicate trouble coming, usually caused by someone else. There may be delays and arguments.

***Hagel*** ᚺ

Don't be in a hurry when Hagel appears, it is the rune of delay and limitation. It represents everything that we are not in control of. Disruptions are likely. If you are thinking of taking a gamble on a situation, think again if Hagel has appeared, the gamble will not pay off. It can show us that our destinies right then are not in our own hands. It is not a time for new beginnings.

If the rest of the runecast is positive, this will have a lessening effect on Hagel, interruptions are likely rather than major disruptions in your life.


## Nid ⼳

How patient are you? Hm? You will need patience if Nid appears. It is the major rune of delay, ill health or constraint of some kind. Don't panic though, you just need to wait it out, things will come good again. Believe it and hang on. Any new projects begun now are doomed from the start, hold your horses and wait until Nid doesn't appear in your runecast. It can be the rune of the drama queen, indicating the possibility of making a drama out of a crisis.

Negatively, Nid implores us not to make any decisions or judgements at this time. It warns against the dangers of impatience. If we act now without waiting for Nid to pass we will only have to do it all over again.


## Is |

Is (ice) means what it sounds like. Freeze, buster. Do nothing, make no sudden moves, don't even blink! It can indicate the cooling off in a relationship, or ask you to recognise the need for a cooling off period before you sign on the dotted line for anything. It can indicate disloyalty, either from another or on your part.

Negatively, in the case of the rest of the runecast being negative, this ice-up is likely to be past rescue. Move on to another project, relationship, job, whatever.


### Ger ᚷ

Hey, a good rune comes along! Ger is the rune of the harvest, of reaping rewards for your efforts. These can be spiritual rewards or material depending on what is going on in your life right at that moment. It is the Justice card of the Tarot, and can indicate legalities or contracts which will be good or bad depending on the rest of the runecast. Harvest time can only happen after ploughing, planting, tending and caring for whatever it is we wish to see come to fruition, in other words everything has a season and your rewards may take some time in coming, but come they will. Have faith. In a dilemma, Ger tells us that all will be well in the end, and can indicate the need for legal assistance

Negatively, Ger asks us to refrain from speaking ill of other people, especially if we don't know the whole story.


### Eoh ᛇ

Never fear, Eoh is here. This is the rune of greatest protection. If your goals and desires are reasonable you will have no problems in attaining them, even delays will be beneficial. Even in the bleakest of times, Eoh in your runecast promises that things will turn out OK. Look to the future at any forthcoming situations. Are they a bit iffy? If so, with Eoh in your runecast things will turn out right if you anticipate the problems and act accordingly.

Eoh is another rune that is difficult to associate with negativity. If the rest of the runecast is a little dodgy, then Eoh will soften this somewhat and lessen the negative interpretation of the other runes.

## Peorth ⌈

Peorth is the rune of the hearth, the home rune. It is also the secret rune, the mystery, things that are hidden. In a runecast, Peorth brings things to light that had previously remained in the shadows. It can really mean the discovery of a secret or it may represent an opportunity that has been 'brewing' in the background and unnoticed. Unexpected gains and nice surprises are forecast with Peorth. This rune is also the rune of the occult, indicating that the questioner has a natural ability in this area.

Negative aspects of Peorth tell of unpleasant surprises. Sometimes it can indicate that someone is about to rattle the skeletons in your closet and bring them out for an airing. Be careful. In connection with the occult, when reversed Peorth can warn of dabbling in what you don't fully understand or when we don't understand our own motivations for using these powerful forces. Don't take a sledgehammer to crack a nut. If lighting a candle or brewing a cuppa will do the trick, don't try invoking powerful entities. For a start it will tick them off, and believe me, we don't want that, and secondly it's a waste of our magickal energy.

## Eolh ↑

Eolh heralds a favourable new influence coming our way. It could be a new career opportunity or the option of a course of new study. It is also the rune of friendship. Strong protective energies surround Eolh which will shield us through the period covered by the reading. Any negative influences or misfortunes are likely to be shown to us in the form of a premonition at this time and so we can take steps to avoid the situation coming to pass. This a cool dude rune bringing benefits to us at this time.

Negative aspects of Eolh show us that we are vulnerable or that we are being asked to sacrifice without attaining anything. Any offers forthcoming at this time should be turned down when Eolh is present in a runecast. You are vulnerable to being used at this time. No new relationships should be formed whilst Eolh shows his face.

### Sigil ⟨

Victory, success, the sun shines down on you right now. This rune is a rune of great power and appearing in an otherwise negative runecast almost negates the negativity of the others. Any obstacles that you have faced will be removed right now. Sometimes Sigil indicates a person who simply has to be in control of their lives and any situation. When this doesn't happen, worry, anxiety and frustration heap up like mountains, this rune tells us to let go and leave the running of the show to others if this is the case.

This rune is another that has no negative position, it is always positive.

### Tir ↑

The winner! Tir guarantees success in any form of competition that we may be involved in. Buy a lottery ticket when this rune appears in your runecast! (Then e mail me with your numbers!) It also indicates a competitive spirit that may not always be apparent. You may get the sudden urge to champion an underdog or set off on a great cause. The gloves are off and you are ready to champion anything that you believe in. Unstoppable is the word that comes to mind and with Sigil on your side, you aren't going down in the first round, you are the champion. Motivation in extremis and a single-mindedness that will not be budged are present now, so go for it honey. You've won before you start. Tir can mean an increase in the old pounds, shillings and pence at this time.

Reversed, oh oh, Tir can bring failure and lack of enthusiasm. Creatively, when Tir is reversed, this is the rune of writer's block, the eternal blank canvas, no stitch on the tapestry. Get the picture?


### Beorc ß

Beorc is the birth rune, the family rune. It may represent your mother or your children, usually indicating joy and family celebrations. It can refer to our spiritual home as opposed to where we live. Any question asked which brings Beorc into the picture will have a satisfactory answer.

When reversed, Beorc may herald family troubles, problems between yourself and your nearest and dearest or simply stress for the ones closest to you.


### Eh ႶႷ

Things are on the move, physically. Maybe a new home or a job relocation. Eh can indicate a shift in opinion but it usually involves physical travel in some form or other. Whether this travel is positive or negative will depend on surrounding runes. You are almost there, the tape is in sight when Eh shows up in a runecast, keep going.

When reversed and amongst other negative runes, don't make any changes at this time, stay home under the duvet.


### Mann ႶႷ

Mann is the rune of the human race or humanity. It is the rune of interdependence on this earth. It tells us that we will receive assistance in times of need. Take any advice you receive at this time. It can warn of becoming too close to a situation to be of value, stand back and let someone else cast some light on the problem. It's a good time for new plans and projects though watch for the presence of delay runes around it. Mann also represents magickal ability.

Reversed, Mann is saying 'You're on your own pal.' Plans will encounter distractions and obstacles now. If this is the case, bide your time until the runes clear. It can also indicate that we can be our own worst enemies and can mean selfishness.


### Lagu ſ

The rune of intuition and inner knowing is Lagu. When it appears in your runecast, abandon logic and act on instinct. Lagu in a cast can also mean that we are receiving spiritual guidance at that time, either consciously or not. Spirit guidance can take the form of dreams and these should be taken seriously at this time. This rune speaks of successful learning or study linked with good memory and imagination.


Oops, Lagu reversed is usually bad mojo, my friend. Unless it is surrounded by positive runes, it usually means that something not quite nice is about to hit the fan. Duck. You are being misled by your intuition and this rune is leading you into muddy waters. It can warn against failing to listening to those inner whispers and rigidly sticking to logic.


### Ing ⌂

Usually a positive rune, Ing heralds the successful completion of all that is at present in hand. Ing appears when an important life event is about to take place, like a birth, marriage, new career etcetera, is in the offing. Good fortune is assured when Ing pops up. It is another rune that really has no negative interpretation, it appears the same whichever way you look at it and whichever way you cut it, Ing is a pretty cool rune to have in your casting.

### Daeg ᛞ

Increase and growth are associated with the rune, Daeg. Again there are no negative aspects to this rune. Daeg counteracts the effect of negative runes that appear with it. Growth is slow and steady but on a firm foundation. Overnight success is not imminent but rather a steady movement forwards that is never going to miss the target. Major changes are sometimes heralded by Daeg, sometimes so mind-blowing that things will never be the same again. New spirituality or new ways of thinking are in the offing when Daeg puts in an appearance.

### Odal ᛟ

Inheritances, family heirlooms, family money are all associated with Odal, the rune of possessions. Tied in with Sigil, the possessions originate through sheer hard work rather than Granny's attic. It can show inherited traits or help from an older family member.

Reversed, Odal is the rune of frustration. It can indicate trying to run before we can walk which is damaging to a project or situation. In this position Odal tells us that we will receive no financial help from family or charitable organisations, we have to sort this one out on our lonesome. The legal system will be of no help either. Ah, well, better get on with it, and hope for a more positive runecast in the not too distant future.

# Reading the Runes

This is known as a runecast. The runes can be drawn from a pouch and laid out in a pattern or they an literally be cast by holding them in your hand and 'throwing the runes onto a cloth or table, even the ground if working outside.

### Three rune cast

Like the three card spread in the Tarot, selecting three runes and placing them one next to the other is used as a quick or basic reading, often in answer to a simple question that could be answered with a yes or no.

### Five rune cast

This is simply and extension of the above runecast, by the addition of two other runes placed directly above and below the centre rune of the above layout. Runes 1,2 and 3 represent past, present and future. The rune above shows any assistance that we are likely to receive and the one below illustrates any aspects of the problem which cannot be altered only accepted.

### Seven rune cast

Beginning at the left hand side, lay six of the runes side by side. The seventh sits underneath and midway between the third and fourth rune.

More complex questions can be asked of this cast, rather than a simple yes or no. In this casting, two runes are read together. The first pair represent the problem or the question, the second pair represent past influences, the third pair show the advice that we are receiving from the runes and the seventh rune, read singly, shows the outcome.

Throwing the runes takes practice to make perfect. If this is the way that you wish to work I recommend that you begin with a casting cloth. Mark on the cloth a large circle showing the four directions, North, East, South and West. Remembering the elemental associations this enable us to tie the positions in with areas of our lives, for example the north (earth) deals with material problems, east (air) intellectual matters, learning, study etc., south (fire) represents changes, transformations, and west throws light on our emotional life. The nearer to the centre of the circle the runes fall the more impact that rune will have on our lives. Any runes that fall outside the circle can be discarded. After some time you will be able to visualise this circle and cast the runes anywhere. This is a method of casting that is most open to our psychic interpretations and prime for development in any way that we wish to create.


## Scrying

Scrying simply involves gazing into a reflective surface. It may be a crystal ball, a dark mirror, a bowl of water or a lake. It is the simplest form of divination and yet can be the hardest to master. It requires us to still our conscious mind and open it to psychic influences and images that we can interpret into something meaningful. This isn't as easy as it sounds but once you have mastered it, it is very effective and very calming. Avoid staring into the object as this produces tension and stilling the conscious mind requires complete relaxation.

There are other methods of divination but those that I have discussed, along with reading the tea leaves, are the methods most often used by the cottage witch.

# 14. Healing

*Sacred scent and magick flower*
*Healing touch at crisis hour.*
*End to sickness in a brew*
*Now the path to health renew.*
*Physical pain or darkest grief*
*The power to heal and bring relief*
*Is in our hands in time of need*
*To share with all, it is decreed.*

It is obviously not within the boundaries of this book that we can explore healing in any great depth, but it wouldn't be complete without at least looking at the different methods of healing that are within the power of the witch. It goes without saying, and I know I have said it before, but I make no apologies for repetition here; all illness that is not of a minor nature or short duration should be referred to qualified medical practitioners, either the G.P. or a trained alternative therapist. To do otherwise would not only be irresponsible but down right dangerous.

This does not mean that we are entirely helpless or that we should stand back and do nothing, the cottage witch certainly wouldn't, and neither would I. There is much we can do simply as compassionate human beings to relieve suffering and help in the recovery process. When sickness is serious and recovery not possible, it is within the realm of the witch to bring peace and comfort and a readiness for the transition to a new state of being. This is healing.

We have already come to discover by now that within us all is an energy that can be used and directed in a positive way, this is magick. The change we wish to bring about in this instance is one of recovery, whether it is physical, spiritual, or mental. By visualisation and the transfer of this energy through our fingertips to the affected person we can deliver healing in its most basic form.

I must point out though, that energy flows in two directions and when giving healing to a really sick person we lay ourselves open to an influx of negative energy as a return flow from the one that is ill. To avoid this we need to protect ourselves. Visualisation of a force-field or energy shield works well here. I have an invisible healing cloak. It is a visualised cloak of vibrant deep blue energy that I 'see' myself flinging around me before I begin any healing.

Whilst we aren't going to contract the illness, unless of course it is of a highly contagious nature, we will feel off colour or out of sorts from absorbing such negative energy if we don't erect some form of psychic barrier, something like a one way tea bag, healing energy can pass through it to the other person but negative energy cannot penetrate it.

After any hands on healing, shake your hands to remove any psychic debris.

### Aromatherapy

The magickal, healing power of scent. For many centuries the essential oils from healing plants have used their power of scent to bring peace and healing on a spiritual and physical level.

Everyday illnesses and traumas can be quite safely treated at home with essential oils that are widely available now in almost every high street. Be aware though, that the cheaper brands may well not be pure essential oils but imitations and while they may smell okay, they don't possess the high vibrational energy that pure essences do.

The oils are used in massage, diluted in a carrier oil such as sunflower or almond oil or they are vaporized using an oil burner. Essential oils can be added to warming baths to bring relaxation or to energise the body.

**Essential oils are generally safe for home use, but a word of caution here, certain oils can be irritant to the skin and can be harmful in pregnancy.** Before using any essential oil please check first that it is safe for use as a home remedy and if anyone that you plan to use the oil on is pregnant, please take professional advice.

### Burns
Neat Lavender oil applied immediately to a minor burn will prevent blistering and remove pain. Anything more severe than a minor burn should be treated by the local casualty unit. Lavender applied neat to sunburn will have the same effect.

### Stress
Stress is one of today's major problems, leading to many serious physical ailments. We all have stress of some degree, the trick is, how we handle it. Relaxation is an art that can take some mastering, but we can help ourselves by using oils in the bath and diffused in an oil burner. Ten drops in the bath and a couple in the burner, of lavender, or basil, or bergamot work wonders for stress.

## Sinusitis

Steam inhalation, you know the picture, head over a bowl of hot water with a towel over the head, works well for this. Five drops in a bowl of hot water are sufficient. Try lemon, eucalyptus or geranium or a blend of all three.

## Rheumatism

This is a condition of cold, so we treat it with warming oils such as black pepper, marjoram or rosemary.

## Painful Periods

No one need suffer painful periods in this day and age, aromatherapy is an excellent remedy for this debilitating condition. Camomile and peppermint or clary sage works wonders, accompanied by a hot water bottle on the tum.

## Insomnia

Everyone goes through this at some time or other, the old brain cells keep whirring and spinning and the ticking of the clock gets louder and louder and you watch the hands go round so painfully slowly. Usually this condition is of fleeting or temporary nature when we have more on our plates than is comfortable. If it is persistent however, we can help ourselves with orange, lavender and sandalwood oils.

## Headaches

Persistent headaches may be a symptom of something else and medical advice should be sought, but the occasional headache brought on by stress or, ha hum, the odd glass of vino too many, or a head cold perhaps, responds very well to lavender oil, rubbed gently into the temples and the nape of the neck. Rosemary oil works well like this too. If the headache is caused by a glass too many of the red stuff, rehydration is important too. Drink gallons of spring or filtered water.

## Colds and 'Flu

Eucalyptus, lemon, lavender, pine, tea tree and thyme, all of these, singly or blended, are the ones to reach for when you feel lousy with a cold.

## Bach Flower Remedies

These natural remedies work on a persons state of mind and spiritual imbalance rather than on a physical level. This means that it is the cause of the illness that is treated rather than its physical manifestation, a far superior way to tackle the problem.

These remedies are available in almost every health food chain on the High Street and are even appearing in mainstream chemists. They aren't prohibitively expensive either and are pleasant to take.

## Rescue Remedy

This Bach Flower Remedy is a combination of some of the main flower remedies and it really does what it says. Four or five drops directly under the tongue in any crisis, minor or major reduces the impact of the emergency of emotional trauma almost immediately. It won't interfere with any conventional medical treatment given in accident centres or by paramedics either. I never leave home without a bottle in my handbag.

**Herbal Remedies**

We have touched on this in Witchin' In The Kitchen, and there are many specialised books on the market that go into greater detail that are excellent sources of information. Suffice it to say that in addition to Herbal Teas and Infusions, it is very easy to make ointments and tinctures at home too. Pre-packed herbal remedies are now available in great numbers in most High Street supermarkets.

The power of touch is incredible and one of the most effective remedies for all minor ailments is a good old fashioned hug and cuddle. Don't be afraid to put your arm around someone who is in pain or upset, it works wonders, costs nothing, and always makes you feel better too. A crying child will always respond to a cuddle, and we are all children deep inside when we are afraid or in pain, and like the upset child, we all respond to a loving arm around us.

# 15.  End Bits

*Our journey's almost over and yet it's just begun*
*We've been inside the cottage with the witchy one*
*We've drunk her tea and stroked her cat*
*Beside the range on the old rag mat*
*Her words of wisdom we still can hear*
*And now we know there's naught to fear*
*In letting out the witch inside*
*'Hey, I'm a Witch', we say with pride.*
*So stir your pots and pans with love*
*And magick sent down from above*
*Use what you have to magick make*
*And cast your spells while bread you bake*
*See what's to come in leaves of tea*
*Hang garlic to make all evil flee*
*But most of all this lesson learn*
*A curse will make your fingers burn*
*So make your magick and have fun*
*Send out your spell but harm no-one*
*So close her door and say adieu*
*To the witchy one who calls to you*
*But you take her with you as you leave*
*To carry on her ways and her magick weave.*

## Familiars

A familiar is a wild animal or domesticated pet such as a cat, dog, rabbit, bird etcetera that has made its home with a witch. This animal is often very responsive to spell working and usually puts in appearance when there's magick in the air, my mog Solstice can sense a witching session from a mile off and she always puts in an appearance. In days gone by, it was enough to send you to the gallows if you were suspected of being a witch and you had a cat!

One thing though, this arrangement has to be on the terms of the animal, it is not ethical to go out and buy a cat or dog to act as an accessory to your magickal tools and paraphernalia. Familiars are very special animals and will appear when they are meant too.

It isn't unusual for a familiar to move on after a while, especially cat familiars. This isn't ingratitude or fear it's usually because another witch needs the help of the familiar more.

## The Law

The Witchcraft Act was repealed in 1951, yes as recently as that. This means that it is no longer against the law to practice witchcraft or to enjoy pagan spirituality. However, The Craft is still not widely accepted and still engenders all kinds of negative emotions and actions so don't expect everyone to pat you on the back and tell you its brilliant that you are a witch, they won't. Many witches keep their practices and spirituality to themselves or between the four walls of their home for this reason. There is however, a middle ground, whereby your 'individuality' can creep out a little at a time. without causing too many ripples. People soon get used to you being 'a little odd' and even find it interesting. Whichever way you choose to deal with your new found art, respect it and live it. You will probably find that based on the principle of sympathetic magick that like attracts like, you will probably find new friends gravitating to you with the same or similar beliefs and lifestyle.

## Best Days

Each day of the week is directly associated with a planet. Each of the planets has a direct link to specific fields of magickal need, for example, Venus is associated with love, so love spells are particularly favoured on the day that corresponds to Venus, which is Friday. Below is a table of the days of the week and their planetary correspondences. This doesn't mean that we have to wait for the specific day, it just adds extra energy to the spell. In times of need, especially in crisis situations, it doesn't make sense to wait, but it can't hurt to repeat the spell on the appropriate day.

| Day of the Week | Planet | Magical Properties |
|---|---|---|
| **Sunday** | Sun | Ambition, success, beginnings, wealth and prosperity and breaking a run of bad luck. |
| **Monday** | Moon | The home, family matters especially Mothers, fertility and psychic development. |
| **Tuesday** | Mars | Courage, fighting injustice, standing up for loved ones. |
| **Wednesday** | Mercury | Communication, orthodox medicine, Business, getting rid of debt, counteracting envy and malice. |
| **Thursday** | Jupiter | Increase and growth, creativity, prosperity and abundance. |
| **Friday** | Venus | Love, harmony and peace, garden spells and women's health. |
| **Saturday** | Saturn | Endings, psychic protection, finding missing objects or lost pets. |

# Best Nights

The phases of the moon can be an effective aid to magickal purpose, but as with selecting the best day, if you need to work a spell in a hurry, then do it. It doesn't make sense to wait almost a month for the right moon phase to come around again, but the spell can be repeated at the right phase of the Moon.

| | |
|---|---|
| **Waxing Moon** | Increase spells of all kinds. Gain in any aspect of your life. Matters concerning young children  or young adults. New beginnings. |
| **Full Moon** | Spells concerning completion, motherhood, energy, fertility, money healing, career. |
| **Waning** | Banishings, getting rid of any negativity, spells of decrease, weight loss. Removing pain and illness, letting go, ending  relationships |
| **Dark** | Spells involving the elderly, especially women, invoking the Dark Goddesses, requiem rites. |

# Trees

| Trees | Magical Associations |
|---|---|
| **Birch** | New beginnings, cleansing |
| **Rowan** | Protection and giving 'sight' |
| **Willow** | Female aspects, the moon |
| **Ash** | Linking inner and outer worlds |
| **Hawthorn** | Protection, cleansing |
| **Oak** | Strength, solid protection |
| **Holly** | Strength in a battle or fight |
| **Hazel** | Intuition |
| **Apple** | Beauty and a link with the Otherworld |
| **Blackthorn** | Cleansing |
| **Elder** | Spirits of witches live in elder, endings and beginnings |
| **Yew** | Rebirth |
| **Beech** | Old knowledge, writing |

In closing, I hope that this little book has been of help to you and that it has brought the Cottage Witch into sharper focus. I hope she becomes your friend as she is mine. Whenever you feel the need, wander down her garden path and you will find that her door is open and she's waiting for you in her warm, cosy kitchen. I expect her cauldron will be on the fire and the kettle singing on her hob ready for the brew that will lift you, comfort you, bring clarity to any problems or maybe show you something good in the tea leaves.

Blessed Be.

# FREE DETAILED CATALOGUE

Capall Bann is owned and run by people actively involved in many of the areas in which we publish. A detailed illustrated catalogue is available on request, SAE or International Postal Coupon appreciated. **Titles can be ordered direct from Capall Bann, post free in the UK** (cheque or PO with order) or from good bookshops and specialist outlets.

A Breath Behind Time, Terri Hector
Angels and Goddesses - Celtic Christianity & Paganism, M. Howard
Arthur - The Legend Unveiled, C Johnson & E Lung
Astrology The Inner Eye - A Guide in Everyday Language, E Smith
Auguries and Omens - The Magical Lore of Birds, Yvonne Aburrow
Asyniur - Womens Mysteries in the Northern Tradition, S McGrath
Beginnings - Geomancy, Electional Astrology, Nigel Pennick
Between Earth and Sky, Julia Day
Book of the Veil , Peter Paddon
Caer Sidhe - Celtic Astrology and Astronomy, Vol 1, Michael Bayley
Caer Sidhe - Celtic Astrology and Astronomy, Vol 2 M Bayley
Call of the Horned Piper, Nigel Jackson
Cat's Company, Ann Walker
Celtic Faery Shamanism, Catrin James
Celtic Lore & Druidic Ritual, Rhiannon Ryall
Celtic Sacrifice - Pre Christian Ritual & Religion, Marion Pearce
Circle and the Square, Jack Gale
Compleat Vampyre - The Vampyre Shaman, Nigel Jackson
Creating Form From the Mist - The Wisdom of Women in Celtic Myth and
      Culture, Lynne Sinclair-Wood
Crystal Clear - A Guide to Quartz Crystal, Jennifer Dent
Crystal Doorways, Simon & Sue Lilly
Crossing Borderlines - Guising, Masking & Ritual Animal Disguise , Nigel Pennick
Dragons of the West, Nigel Pennick
Earth Dance - A Year of Pagan Rituals, Jan Brodie
Earth Harmony - Places of Power, Holiness & Healing, Nigel Pennick
Earth Magic, Margaret McArthur
Eildon Tree (The) Romany Language & Lore, Michael Hoadley
Enchanted Forest - The Magical Lore of Trees, Yvonne Aburrow
Eternal Priestess, Sage Weston
Eternally Yours Faithfully, Roy Radford & Evelyn Gregory
Everything You Always Wanted To Know About Your Body, But So Far
      Nobody's Been Able To Tell You, Chris Thomas & D Baker

Fairies in the Irish Tradition, Molly Gowen
Familiars - Animal Powers of Britain, Anna Franklin
Forest Paths - Tree Divination, Brian Harrison, Ill. S. Rouse
Gardening For Wildlife Ron  Wilson
God Year, The, Nigel Pennick & Helen Field
Goddess on the Cross, Dr George Young
Goddess Year, The, Nigel Pennick & Helen Field
Goddesses, Guardians & Groves, Jack Gale
Handbook For Pagan Healers, Liz Joan
Handbook of Fairies, Ronan Coghlan
Healing Book, The, Chris Thomas and Diane Baker
Healing Homes, Jennifer Dent
Healing Journeys, Paul Williamson
Healing Stones, Sue Philips
Herb Craft - Shamanic & Ritual Use of Herbs,  Lavender  & Franklin
In Search of Herne the Hunter, Eric Fitch
Inner Celtia, Alan Richardson & David Annwn
Journey Home, The, Chris Thomas
Legend of Robin Hood, The, Richard Rutherford-Moore
Lid Off the Cauldron, Patricia Crowther
Light From the Shadows - Modern Traditional Witchcraft, Gwyn
Living Tarot, Ann Walker
Lore of the Sacred Horse, Marion Davies
Lost Lands & Sunken Cities (2nd ed.), Nigel Pennick
Magic of Herbs - A Complete Home Herbal, Rhiannon Ryall
Magical Guardians - Exploring the Spirit and Nature of Trees,  Philip Heselton
Magical History of the Horse, Janet Farrar & Virginia Russell
Magical Lore of Animals, Yvonne Aburrow
Magical Lore of Cats, Marion Davies
Magical Lore of Herbs, Marion Davies
Magick Without Peers, Ariadne Rainbird & David Rankine
Masks of Misrule - Horned God & His Cult in Europe, Nigel Jackson
Mirrors of Magic - Evoking the Spirit of the Dewponds, P Heselton
Moon Mysteries, Jan Brodie
Mysteries of the Runes, Michael Howard
Mystic Life of Animals, Ann Walker
New Celtic Oracle The,  Nigel Pennick & Nigel Jackson
Pagan Feasts - Seasonal Food for the 8 Festivals, Franklin & Phillips
Patchwork of Magic  - Living in a Pagan World, Julia Day
Pathworking - A Practical Book of Guided Meditations, Pete Jennings
Personal Power, Anna Franklin
Pickingill Papers - The Origins of Gardnerian Wicca, Bill Liddell
Pillars of Tubal Cain, Nigel Jackson
Practical Divining, Richard Foord
Practical Meditation, Steve Hounsome
Psychic Self Defence - Real Solutions, Jan Brodie

Real Fairies, David Tame
Reality - How It Works & Why It Mostly Doesn't, Rik Dent
Romany Tapestry, Michael Houghton
Runic Astrology, Nigel Pennick
Sacred Animals, Gordon MacLellan
Sacred Celtic Animals, Marion Davies, Ill. Simon Rouse
Sacred Dorset - On the Path of the Dragon, Peter Knight
Sacred Grove - The Mysteries of the Forest, Yvonne Aburrow
Sacred Geometry, Nigel Pennick
Sacred Nature, Ancient Wisdom & Modern Meanings, A Cooper
Sacred Ring - Pagan Origins of British Folk Festivals, M. Howard
Season of Sorcery - On Becoming a Wisewoman, Poppy Palin
Seasonal Magic - Diary of a Village Witch, Paddy Slade
Secret Places of the Goddess, Philip Heselton
Secret Signs & Sigils, Nigel Pennick
Spirits of the Earth series, Jaq D Hawkins
Stony Gaze, Investigating Celtic Heads John Billingsley
Stumbling Through the Undergrowth , Mark Kirwan-Heyhoe
Subterranean Kingdom, The, revised 2nd ed, Nigel Pennick
Symbols of Ancient Gods, Rhiannon Ryall
Talking to the Earth, Gordon MacLellan
Taming the Wolf - Full Moon Meditations, Steve Hounsome
Teachings of the Wisewomen, Rhiannon Ryall
Tree: Essence of Healing, Simon & Sue Lilly
Torch and the Spear, Patrick Regan
Understanding Chaos Magic, Jaq D Hawkins
Warriors at the Edge of Time, Jan Fry
Water Witches, Tony Steele
Way of the Magus, Michael Howard
Weaving a Web of Magic, Rhiannon Ryall
West Country Wicca, Rhiannon Ryall
Wildwitch - The Craft of the Natural Psychic, Poppy Palin
Witches of Oz, Matthew & Julia Philips
Wondrous Land - The Faery Faith of Ireland by Dr Kay Mullin
Working With the Merlin, Geoff Hughes

# FREE detailed catalogue and FREE 'Inspiration' magazine

## Contact: Capall Bann Publishing, Auton Farm, Milverton, Somerset, TA4 1NE